Praise for

"Steve Centore is that noblest of citizens: the honest witness. After a career of quiet public service, his greatest act of public service is to not be quiet at all, exposing how the government covered up the deadly health consequences of working at Ground Zero in the months following the 9/11 attack. Centore has endured life threatening ostracization for speaking out, but this book and his heroism in writing it will outlive the wretched shame it illuminates."

—**Bob Guccione, Jr., Chairman of *DISCOVER***

"With unflinching honesty, this troubling memoir depicts a case of Post Traumatic Stress Disorder tragically ignored by the US government.

After serving in the Navy, Centore joined the DOE to direct a team charged with investigating possible incidents of [radiation] contamination. During the months following 9/11, Centore worked at Ground Zero, searching the wreckage for radioactive materials.

Upon being diagnosed with PTSD, the government accused him of going AWOL and milking the system with illegitimate claims about his health.

In the final stages of giving this account, the author became so ill that he had to turn narrative duties over to his wife, Sue. The dual narration gives the memoir a stunning immediacy.

The forceful subject matter compels all on its own. Flashing back to his hardscrabble childhood in Havelock, N.C., Centore investigates the dynamics of a family devoted to the military, including a father and stepfather, both Marines. Time spent on a nuclear submarine during the waning years of the Cold War instilled in the author a devoted, diligent work ethic. When Centore found himself abandoned by his country, he had to reinvent his life; the dedicated, stoic patriot became a passionate, rebellious crusader. This transformation, vividly rendered, forms the dynamic heart of the book. Details about Navy racism, government bureaucracy and the mechanics of an underwater vessel serve as fascinating extras.

An important story that deserves to be heard."

—*Kirkus Discoveries*

"As one of Steve's ex-colleagues in the submarine service, I can tell you he is a good man that has suffered much while gladly serving his country during a lifetime of service. He deserves to be heard. Please listen."

—**Julius Bryant, Nuclear Power Plant Manager
and Crew Member of USS Seahorse**

"Immediately after 9/11, America embraced the heroism, daring, and caring of everyone involved in the rescue and recovery at Ground Zero. Now, many people like Steve Centore are being betrayed and forgotten by our government. As a Vietnam Vet, I watched as a previous generation turned its back on the gallant men and women who suffered the horrors of poisons like Agent Orange and the medical and emotional trauma of war. Well, it's happened again. But today, by shouting the truth, patriots like Steve Centore are fighting a new war on the home front to preserve America's values and prevent the politicians and media from abandoning their commitment to our newest generation of heroes."

—John Ketwig, author of
...and a hard rain fell: A G.I's True Story of the Vietnam War

"After working with you at Brookhaven, as I watched you cope with your responsibilities with the RAP team, I was consistently impressed with your dedication and ability to work with the many personalities and challenges you faced every day. No easy task. What a fun time we had when Bev, Billy and I shared dinner with you and Susan, your beautiful bride-to-be, at the top of the WTC but who would have guessed what was to come. I'm saddened at what has happened to your health. I hope your voice is heard. God Bless."

—William King, Disaster Preparedness Officer,
Department of Homeland Security; Master Chief (US Navy Retired)

"As you know I served in the British Army and saw duty in the cold back streets of Northern Ireland and feel very disheartened that our governments have ignored those who serve and place their lives on the wire. The loss of your services to the US government is their loss and through the will of God you will prevail and your voice will be heard. Only those that have served their country will understand the pain and betrayal you feel. Keep your voice loud and proud."

—David J Cackett, Operational Manager, Sun Microsystems

"I hadn't heard about your health nor your fine efforts. That's true to who you are. For it is people like us who toil in silence for the greater good, expecting neither gratitude nor thanks with our sole belief being what we do makes a difference—which is why I am so appalled when our government acts with such callous duplicitousness with regard to those who serve."

—Jude M. Clark, President and CEO, DyLog Associates

Awards Presented to the Author

"Presented to Steven M. Centore: In recognition of your assistance to New York City following the attack on the World Trade Center, September 11, 2001. Your role in the successful response of the Radiological Assistance Program Team and the Fire Department from the U. S. Department of Energy's Brookhaven National Laboratory demonstrated your dedication to your profession, the Department of Energy, the City of New York, the State of New York, and the United States of America."

— Spencer Abraham, Secretary of Energy

"A Certificate of Special Congressional Recognition (is) presented to Steve Centore in support of World Trade Center Operations, in recognition of outstanding and invaluable service to the community."

—Congressman Felix Grucci

"Presented to Steven M. Centore: In recognition of the efforts made toward revitalizing Brookhaven Area Office (BRO) participation in the Radiological Assistance Program (RAP) as the Region One Coordinating Office. Your display of professionalism in reestablishing effective working relationships with federal, state, and local emergency response organizations has been critical to BHO meeting its RAP responsibilities."

—Cherri J. Langenfeld, Manager, DOE

ONE
OF
THEM
A First Responder's Story

Steven M. Centore

Worldwide Association of Disabled Veterans, Inc.

For further information, please contact:
scentore@yahoo.com
wadv-oneofthem.com

Book design by:
ARBOR BOOKS, INC.
19 Spear Road, Suite 301
Ramsey, NJ 07446
www.arborbooks.com

Printed in the United States of America

One of Them: A Firts Responder's Story
Steven M. Centore
1. Title 2. Author 3. Memoir

Library of Congress Control Number: 2007940621

ISBN-10: 0-9801274-0-8
ISBN-13: 978-0-9801274-0-9

To my mother, who has always believed in me.
Virginia Elizabeth McCann Bell
From one of your roses

DEDICATION

I would like to dedicate this book to my best friend, who just happens to be my wife, Susan Madeline Jones Centore. You see, she is more than my life, I owe her my life. When it seemed it was just you and me and the future was looking bleak, you were determined not to give in, never give up, and never say good-bye.

When I think about you I remember the line from a song that goes, *Heaven must have sent you, honey.* You are my angel, my heart, my life. I will love you forever. Your adoring husband, GP.

ACKNOWLEDGEMENTS

There are certainly many people who I have met throughout my life that have in someway made an impact on me and my ideals. At this time I would like to acknowledge my mother, Virginia, who has always been in my heart no matter where life's path has taken me.

My sisters, Debbie, Terri, Cherie, and Missy, who have always let me know and made me feel comfortable in the knowledge that no matter what happens out in the world, I always had a place to come home to where, everything aside, we were still family and we had each other.

To Maddy and Milt, my in-laws. You are two of the kindest and warmest people I have ever met. You accepted me into your home as one of your own. I believe you know how Sue and I feel about the two of you.

To Kenny and Marie, my brother-in-law and his wife. You guys have always been there when we needed a helping hand, especially in the worst of times.

To my wife's other siblings, Billy, Katy, and Pam; Aunts Rita and Kay; my cousins Pete, John, Michael, Janice, and their spouses, I wanted to personally thank you for your support and prayers.

To all my brothers from the USS Seahorse, those still here and those on eternal patrol. This was the closest thing to a family I ever had after I left home.

To all my friends and co-workers at DOE/NNSA and Brookhaven Lab. It has been one hell of a wild ride, just watch out for the train wreck at the end.

To all my friends whom I served with in our country's war on terror. I would especially like to thank Pete Grossgold for not only being my partner, but also one of my dearest friends.

To my friends of FDNY's HazMat Unit One and those who perished in the terrible events of 9/11/2001. You will always be in my thoughts and prayers.

I especially want to thank Dr. Lewis Teperman and his staff at the NYU Transplant Clinic in NYC, my primary physician, Dr. Luigi Buono, and also to Drs. Melissa Palmer, Eyad Ali, Edwin Sause and Marilyn McLaughlin.

To a special person whom I have never met but who gave me a very precious gift, God bless you and I hope to meet you on the other side.

And finally, to my children, Christina, Chuck, Courtney, and Steven. I love you all very much, you are my life. The sacrifices I have made for you are known only to me and God.

PREFACE

L ike most people who have served their country, I don't think of myself as heroic, or remarkable or superior in any way to my fellow Americans. Those of us who serve the greater good do so out of a sense of service, not a need to separate ourselves. Nevertheless, service to one's country brings feelings of pride as well as camaraderie with one's co-workers. We think of ourselves as the good guys, those who protect the country we love, not only for ourselves and our families and friends, but for everyone. That dedication and the ordeals many of us go through bond us for life. It creates a brotherhood that's exclusive of the rest of the world.

And then we find ourselves needing help, or raising concerns, or overtly criticizing bad decisions—not because we're opposed to the system, but because we *care* about the system—at times valuing loyalty and duty over our own well-being. And suddenly we find ourselves ousted from the brotherhood; ignored, dismissed and denigrated by the people we had dedicated our lives to serving.

It's as though our service to country had been eliminated from our permanent record. We go from being One of Us, the good guys, to being One of Them, the critics, the malingerers, the troublemakers. Even though our belief in the system hasn't wavered, the system has opted to reject us because we no longer conform, even though conforming may now be beyond our capability.

I always thought of myself as One of Us and served my country with pride and distinction. I'm now One of Them, cast aside because the problems I wanted addressed, according to some people in the government, don't exist. They've opted to kill the messenger in my case. Yet, I'm in good company, I suppose, because the ranks of Them has been steadily growing in recent years, and it includes some very important people.

But there's sadness, too, that after a lifetime of selfless service I was discarded at the first sign of trouble, trouble beyond my ability to control. I didn't want to be this guy; I would have continued on in the service of my country indefinitely, given the opportunity. But that ship has sailed.

I know I'll never be One of Us again.

This is my story.

CHAPTER 1

It was in July, 2005 when I had my first panic attack, or so I was told, because I have no memory of it or of any of them. The attacks would come on so quickly and without warning and last indefinitely, sometimes with profound consequences. During one of them my wife found me sitting in the driveway in the middle of the night, staring off into space.

It was after the panic attacks started that I recalled how after several nearly sleepless, physically and mentally draining weeks working on the pile at Ground Zero we were given a one half hour briefing with a psychologist. "Years from now you might be going about your business and you'll have a traumatic flashback, but don't worry, it's just a delayed psychological effect," we were told.

We brushed off the warning. *That can't happen to us*, we thought. And now it was happening to me.

On Sept. 12, 2005, two months after my first panic attack, I was diagnosed with Post Traumatic Stress Disorder (PTSD), four years to the day after I arrived on the pile at Ground Zero.

I was sitting in the examining room of my physician, Dr. Luigi Buono, when the diagnosis was made, but I didn't react to the news because I was in the midst of another panic attack. My body tensed up, my eyes went vacant, my skin went pale and my breathing became shallow. And I mercifully was unaware of everything happening to me, as I always was.

Dr. Buono was startled, but immediately recognized the attack for what it was. My wife, Sue, had experienced the sight of me freezing up many times before—not that it was ever easy.

I remember driving to the doctor's office, and the next thing I was aware of was me on my way home in the car, and my wife was stopping at the pharmacy to fill the doctor's prescriptions for Xanax and Zoloft.

I had never even heard of PTSD before I was diagnosed with it, but I came to learn that it's a psychological response to exposure to extremely stressful events a person experiences as highly traumatic. Ground Zero certainly qualified as highly traumatic, though I didn't feel its effects immediately.

But PTSD was only the beginning of the problems I was about to endure, the legacy of my four months working for the Department of Energy (DOE) at the site of the attacks on the World Trade Center.

CHAPTER 2

I'd experienced the first serious physical symptom of what was to come in May, 2005, when I was going to Washington to visit DOE's headquarters. I twisted my back boarding the Amtrak train in Penn Station in New York City. I could barely move, but eventually I managed to turn around and return home.

My job at the time was leading a Radiological Assistance Program Team (RAP) in the northeastern United States, searching for possible radiological hot spots.

After my four month tour at Ground Zero my team and I were assigned to assist the Nuclear Emergency Support Team (NEST) to search for and analyze potential nuclear/radiological threats. Despite our initial lack of training on the assorted NEST equipment and the fact that we'd worked non-stop since the 9/11 terrorist attacks including several months in support to the national NEST Team, we were given the lead role for monitoring and evaluating potential radioactive attacks on the United States.

I hadn't been feeling right for several months—nothing specific, just an overall sense of feeling ill. The injury was unexpected; I'd never hurt my back before. The pain was unbearable, like nothing I had ever experienced. I visited Dr. Buono, who diagnosed me with a herniated disc and prescribed a seven-day bed rest and Tylenol with codeine, which left me in a stupor for the week. I didn't know at the time that I was allergic to codeine, but it did alleviate the pain.

I had accrued so much vacation and sick time during my time with DOE that taking time away from my job wasn't an issue, though the reasons for my time away were about to become an issue for my supervisors at Brookhaven National Laboratory on Long Island, where I was based.

After a week off to recuperate from my back injury, I returned to my duties, still not feeling well but determined to continue working.

I'd been telling my Division Manager at Brookhaven that I wasn't feeling well for several months, but he dismissed my complaints. My chain of command was convoluted: I received my marching orders from the DOE brass in Washington, D.C., but personnel issues were handled by my superiors close to home at Brookhaven.

Then came the panic attacks, nearly four years after my 9/11 assignment, and they increased dramatically with each passing month. One attack occurred when I was socializing with my wife, Sue, her brother and his wife. The weather was beautiful and we were out on the deck listening to a band play, looking out over the water, drinking beer and relaxing, and suddenly I was aware that Sue and her sister were rubbing my arms, telling me I was going to be all right.

I didn't know what had happened, but apparently I'd become catatonic and pale, and when I came out of it I'd gone from being in a festive mood to being exhausted and filled with unease. That was typical of what I experienced during the panic attacks.

Their frequency escalated to the point that I was barely finished with one when the next one would start. I was missing a lot of time at work, as was Sue, who came home from work a number of times to find me catatonic. She was increasingly afraid to leave me alone, and I was increasingly afraid of jeopardizing my or someone else's safety.

The only exception that summer was the week in August I took to visit my mother in Illinois. I hadn't seen her in four or five years, and I badly needed the break. I spent the entire week just relaxing and socializing in a rural setting, not thinking about work, and I didn't have a single episode. When I returned home and resumed working, the panic attacks resumed as well, with a vengeance.

Something in my mind was going terribly wrong.

CHAPTER 3

The genesis of my problems can be traced to one gigantic, horrifying event: 9/11

Ground Zero, Sept. 12, 2001: I'm standing amidst a pile of rubble so immense it's incomprehensible, and it's being carried out in white plastic buckets. White plastic buckets, handed man to man, a gallon or two at a time, to remove the remains of two enormous skyscrapers and thousands of human beings.

The dust is a choking yellow haze, and you can see only several feet in front of you. The dust settles on everything, two inches thick in most places, and it's like walking on the moon. The overwhelming awe I'm feeling is almost indescribable, but the thousands of workers are there to rescue survivors, if there are any, so focusing on that task is of primary importance.

As if there could possibly be any survivors in this smoldering cataclysm.

As Regional Response Coordinator for the Department of Energy's Radiological Assistance Program, I'm there with my team to find radioactive hot spots, and the New York Department of Health has provided us with several potential radiological contaminants housed within the World Trade Center.

Depleted uranium is another concern, not as a radiological problem but as a toxin, as that was used in the older model jets as a counterbalance in the tail.

The twisted steel and pulverized concrete from the towers is mixed with molten pools of aluminum, broken glass, paper and office fixtures, and yes, body parts. The search through the rubble is initially in hopes of finding survivors, but those hopes diminish with each passing day. Much of the work being done by hand serves to remove debris and find human remains, but the human remains are usually horribly fragmented and sometimes unrecognizable as being from a human body.

I pick up what I think is a section of hose only to discover it's an arm. I find a pair of shoes on the sidewalk with the feet still in them.

There are nearly three thousand bodies in this cataclysmic mess, and despite finding thousands of body parts, more than one thousand one hundred people will remain unidentified and permanently interred at Fresh Kills Landfill on Staten Island, which is where the pile from Ground Zero is ultimately dumped.

Several years later I see an anti-smoking ad on television that includes mannequin appendages sticking out of a garbage can, and my response is one of visceral horror. That image is a metaphor for the makers of the commercial, but for me it's a literal memory, one I can't shake.

CHAPTER 4

I had been working at my office at Brookhaven National Laboratory on Long Island on the morning of Sept. 11 when news came that a small plane had struck one of the World Trade Center towers at eight forty-six a.m.

By now the story is horribly familiar, but when the first plane hit we were just getting our coffee and settling in at work, and the initial story was odd, but not terrifying. Early reports were that a single prop plane had struck one of the towers, and this seemed like a plausible event, dangerous but not extreme. I thought, *Well, the towers are big. Other large buildings have been hit by planes in the past, including the Empire State Building. It could happen.*

We went to the conference room and put on the television. Part of our responsibility as an Emergency Response Unit for the DOE was monitoring the networks for breaking news, so we turned on the big screen in the conference room in time to see a second plane crash into the other tower. A jet, not a prop plane, the resulting explosion was phenomenally violent.

"Oh my God, we're under attack," I said.

The local TV stations were down, and a lot of the information coming over the twenty-four-hour news networks was confusing and contradictory, including the report that a car bomb had been detonated at the State Department's headquarters in Washington. It was also reported, for example, that a third hijacked plane had struck the Pentagon, and shortly after came the erroneous report that a fire had broken out on the Washington Mall. Other false reports stated that flight 1989 out of Cleveland had been hijacked, that the Sears Tower was targeted, and that sites in Los Angeles were vulnerable.

In one instance, a news network stated that as many as twelve planes were unaccounted for, and such panicky and incorrect information only added to the sense of dread.

All the local stations had their antennas on the World Trade Center towers and therefore had no signal, but from the national news networks we eventually learned that four commercial airliners had been hijacked en route to California from Logan International Airport in Boston, Newark International (now Liberty) in New Jersey and Dulles International in Washington. There was a sense of helpless horror as we watched the towers burn.

On the television emergency personnel were shepherding people from the towers. People trapped above the fires, which were fueled by thousands of gallons of jet fuel, began jumping to their deaths. Eventually the cameras pulled back and stopped showing the desperate suicides.

And then Tower Two, the south tower which had been struck second by United Airlines flight 175, crashed to the earth at nine fifty-nine a.m. after burning for fifty-six minutes. The fire caused by the plane's impact and thousands of gallons of fuel from it had damaged the tower's infrastructure enough to cause the steel skeleton to collapse, taking down millions of tons of concrete, and everyone and everything inside with it.

I thought, *There's no way that can happen. There's no way.* And then down it went.

The only consolation, and it was of minimal consolation, was that the tower collapsed into itself. When it started to fall I expected a domino effect, a sideways toppling that would take dozens of adjacent buildings and their inhabitants with it. But the tower fell straight down, as it was designed to do.

But even after Tower Two fell, I was convinced Tower One would never fall. It was hit first, it was still standing, and the first collapse was just an anomaly.

Tower One, struck by American flight 11, fell twenty-nine minutes after Tower Two, after burning for one hundred two minutes.

It was later determined that one thousand three hundred sixty-six people died who were at or above the floors of impact in Tower One. Many were killed instantly by the impact, while others were trapped and died when the tower collapsed; approximately six hundred people were killed instantly or trapped at or above the floors of impact in Tower Two.

At least two hundred people jumped from the towers. A number of people in both towers made their way toward the roof in hope of helicopter rescue, but no rescue plan existed for such an evacuation, the roof access doors were locked, and the thick smoke prevented landings on the roofs.

I had fears for the many friends I had working at Tower Seven at the Mayor's Office of Emergency Management, but there were no land lines and limited cell phone reception, and there was an emergency response team to prepare, so I never had the opportunity to call any of them. I didn't even call home initially.

Then there was HazMat One. Part of my assignment as the Regional Response Coordinator was to provide training to local first responders from various organizations from all over the Northeast, and one of these groups was FDNY's Hazardous Material Response Unit One, commonly referred to as HazMat One. We would travel to Randall's Island to train with them at the training facility. We would conduct classroom training followed by a live radioactive source exercise. During this time we had built quite a relationship with them. They were always kidding us about glowing in the dark and stuff like that. But when it came time to eat, they would always invite us to eat with them as they cooked their meals together and ate together in the facility.

I considered it a rare honor to be allowed to dine with them, as one of them. I was accepted as part of their family. This relationship would continue for many years. On 9/11, I learned that one squad of men from HazMat One were killed when the towers collapsed. They died doing what they did best, what they loved to do; saving others. Nowadays, we tend to throw the term "hero" around so much that its meaning has been somewhat diluted. I consider these men Real Heroes. I am humbled that they let me become part of their world; and now it is gone…for me…forever.

A fourth hijacked plane, United 93, then crashed in rural Pennsylvania. There were reports that it had been heading for the Capitol building, and that was later confirmed. It was never confirmed that the passengers breached the cockpit, but apparently having learned of the other hijackings on their cell phones the passengers rushed the hijackers, forcing them to crash the plane short of their target.

At five-twenty that afternoon Tower Seven collapsed, structurally damaged by the nearby collapsing Twin Towers. Gone was the city's Office of Emergency Management headquarters.

We fully mobilized to respond, but were then ordered to wait for further instructions from the FBI, who initially requested our support and for our teams to coordinate with their teams. There was nothing more we could do amidst the chaos of the day except stand by.

As team leader, I identified who would work on the team and we gathered our survey meters, air samplers and vehicles.

And then, as is often the case in times of great crisis, we anxiously waited for further orders.

Our role, which was being coordinated with the FBI and the New York City Health Department, would be to identify, evaluate and remediate radioactive hot spots in the aftermath of the towers' collapse. I had been with DOE at Brookhaven for nine years, and we'd had our share of radiological investigations, but this would be the largest operation by far.

Radiation is a scary thing to most people, and its effects can be deadly, but most people overestimate the danger associated with most kinds of radiation; they think with the danger of any radiation exposure that it's necessary to wear lead-lined suits, but doctors giving you X-rays put you under a lead apron for your mental well-being, not your physical care. Medical X-ray procedures aren't dangerous, even thousands of them, and the type of radiation that can kill you won't be stopped by a lead apron, anyway. Our response team used Tyvec, the same material they insulate houses with; it's sufficient to shield several types of harmful radiation, although the suits are worn mainly for contamination control.

Once notified of our responsibility we were ready to go at a moment's notice, but all we could do while we waited was watch as the towers fell, knowing that there were hundreds of emergency responders, people we had worked with and trained, likely lost when those massive steel and cement structures crashed to earth.

I had been in Tower Seven just a week earlier.

CHAPTER 5

It was early evening on Sept. 12 when we arrived at Ground Zero. I had actually sent the team home earlier in the day when we were ordered to stand down, but we were activated again several hours later. "Are you sure this time?" team members asked me, but that decision was beyond my control.

We were finally ordered to move. I can't recall how my team reached Manhattan from Long Island—over one of the bridges, no doubt, which were closed to the public. Our first stop was a meeting at the New York City Department of Health's laboratory on First Avenue for a briefing with the Deputy Commissioner on possible radiological hot spots, which included a radiography source in one of the towers with great potential for dangerous emissions.

We had a van for our equipment and a Jeep Grand Cherokee with a light bar affixed to the roof and a dedicated frequency radio as our command vehicle, which we parked on the corner of Chambers and West Streets. While my team prepared its gear to enter the zone I visited the makeshift emergency operations center, located at a school on Chambers Street, for a briefing with the city's Office of Emergency Management personnel.

I glanced down the street at where the towers had been, but could only get a glimpse through the haze and commotion of what was going on at the site. I didn't dwell on what we were walking into, but I knew it was definitely not somewhere you wanted to be if you didn't have to be there.

In fact, as much as Ground Zero swallowed you up and soon became your only point of reference, the enormity of the devastation wasn't possible to comprehend while on the ground in the middle of it. Only by walking completely around the site would it be possible to see even a fraction of the calamity, but that was unnecessary. We were immersed in it, and overwhelmed by it.

An NYPD Special Operations officer gave us a tour of the site and handed out paper masks and hardhats. We'd bought steel-toed shoes the day before. He warned us that buildings, glass and assorted debris were still falling all around the area, but after flinching at the noise of a partial collapse, I realized it was futile. *Where am I going to run?*

It was like nothing any of us ever had experienced before.

It was impossible to create a search grid for an area so large and so devastated, so we began on the perimeter of the area and worked inward in concentric circles. In addition to surveying the site for radiation we also had the responsibility of taking readings of all the trucks that were hauling away the debris, and they had no intention of waiting for us to scan them for radiation. Trucks were lined up as far as you could see on the West Side Highway, and at one point they opened a second route out of the city for the dump trucks without telling us, but we quickly established a second survey team at the new location.

A front loader was already on site, scooping up debris, but the irony of the cleanup was that it was also a crime scene with thousands of bodies in it, so there was an ostensible effort to find remains while at the same time there was an effort to clean up the site as quickly as possible.

I wasn't accustomed to operations running that way, but it wasn't my operation. Nevertheless, there was this sense that we were fumbling through, that chaos was the governing principle in the entire process.

I rotated team members in and out, and encouraged everyone to take regular breaks and report back to our command post at the vehicles. Still, the experience was consistently mind-numbing and overwhelming.

One day a reporter from a French TV station asked me if it was time to stop looking for survivors. At first I declined to answer, but under pressure, I responded, "If it was your friends out there, would you stop?" After that he left me alone.

Fresh emergency personnel were always coming in to assist in the cleanup, so one minute you'd be working in an area, trying to stay out of the way of the cleanup personnel, and the next there'd be a new National Guard unit in that sector, questioning your right to be working there. But the FBI, with whom we were coordinating our work, never questioned us on our progress, which was fine with me and the rest of our team. We were professionals who knew how to do our jobs and didn't require a lot of oversight.

When we were working on the pile, a whistle would blast once to signal everyone to stop working because someone thought they heard something, but after several days the hope of finding survivors faded, and that whistle blew less and less frequently.

The whistle was also blasted three times when there was danger of falling debris; pieces of the buildings and broken glass continually crashed to the ground. In addition to the Twin Towers and Seven World Trade Center, other severely damaged buildings in the neighborhood included the two New York City subway stations and St. Nicholas Greek Orthodox Church. In total, twenty-five buildings were damaged in the attacks and all seven buildings of the World Trade Center complex were eventually razed.

Two other buildings were condemned and razed several years later: the Deutsche Bank Building and Manhattan Community College's Fiterman Hall.

One time they blasted the warning whistle three times, and we looked to see that the Marriott Millennium on Broadway, which was covered in black glass, was swaying. We ran like scared rabbits only to realize that you can't outrun a falling skyscraper. We were later told a few panels of glass fell off the building, but the building never collapsed.

Eventually it was declared structurally sound and it reopened, but there's no way I'd ever stay in that hotel.

There was also the danger of the pile itself, where an intense fire burned for ninety-nine days, jagged metal and glass was everywhere, and sinkholes would open up under your feet. Beneath the visible World Trade Center were numerous sub-levels that included underground sections of the towers, subway stations and utility levels, and the support structures for these levels had also been demolished by the collapse.

I saw a fireman who had fallen through the debris he was working on and into a hole; he had to be dug out, and he was white as a ghost from all the ash he'd been lying in.

Those of us working at Ground Zero were mostly oblivious to what was going on in the outside world in those first weeks. For one thing, we couldn't leave, and because of all the downed lines and towers, we mostly couldn't communicate with the outside world. We knew that commercial planes were grounded for several days, but in terms of knowing who was responsible or what our government's reaction was to the attack, we were too absorbed by the task at hand to worry much about external issues.

All that mattered was sorting through the ruin where the towers had been.

I worked part of the time on the pile, part of the time in the makeshift emergency operations center, which had phone lines trailing across the floor. There were only ten lines coming into the entire area, jerry-rigged by a Verizon installer, so there were no personal calls. Everyone wanted to get information from those of us working at Ground Zero, so the phones were lit up at all times.

At one meeting in the EOC I ran into Bob Ingram, who operated the city's Hazmat Unit One, the premiere FDNY hazardous material crew in New York City, looking tired and distraught. I knew Bob from working with him in the past. He told me how when the first tower fell, he and the engine driver ducked under their truck to escape the falling debris. He was practically in tears describing how he'd lost every other man in his unit, all seven men, when the tower fell.

"I need to talk with you when we get a chance," he said. But we never did get to finish the conversation, not for many years to come.

It was later determined that among the nearly three thousand casualties that day were three hundred forty-three New York City firefighters and paramedics, twenty-three New York City police officers, and thirty-seven Port Authority officers. Many of the survivors from that day owe their lives to the emergency responders who herded them from the towers and away from where they would ultimately collapse.

CHAPTER 6

Upon our arrival we were offered cloth masks for respiratory reasons, however, no one had informed us of any specific hazards that might be present. As we continued to work at the pile our cloth masks became clogged with soot, so we removed them in order to breathe. Officials kept telling us the air was fine to breathe and that respirators weren't necessary, but I had my doubts.

I noticed that my arms itched because the silica was sticking to them. Silica was a byproduct of asbestos burning, and there was a lot of asbestos in the towers. There were all these particles in the air, and the fires burned relentlessly for months.

I was even more worried about phosgene, a lethal gas that's produced when freon in air conditioners is burned, and I know the air conditioners in the towers were incinerated along with everything else in the fire. There were any number of particulates and chemicals in that air, and there were survey crews taking samples, but no warning was ever given.

You'd blow your nose and the results were black crud. Your eyes would burn all the time. And always came the reassurances, from EPA Secretary Christine Todd Whitman on down: *The air is fine to breathe. Nothing to worry about.*

We worked non-stop for the first two weeks. Because lower Manhattan was barricaded, it was difficult to leave the site. Initially we didn't sleep at all. I don't remember sleeping for several days after we first arrived. Eventually I got some sleep in my truck, but we were there several weeks before the team was allowed to leave the area.

Some of the emergency responders took furniture out of buildings in the area and set up little living room areas for themselves on the sidewalks. Others had taken to just sleeping directly on the sidewalks. I saw one fireman sleeping in a pile of dust on the sidewalk. I walked over, thinking he was dead, and then I saw him move, which startled me.

We weren't finding any significant radiation, and the city was skeptical of our findings, or lack thereof. But our team was thorough and expert at our jobs.

On Nov. 12 at about nine-sixteen in the morning, American flight 587, crashed into a residential area of Belle Harbor in Queens, jut after taking off from John F. Kennedy International Airport on Long Island. All two hundred sixty people aboard the plane and five people on the ground were killed in the crash, and the plane was destroyed by impact and the post-crash fire. People on the ground reported an explosion just prior to the crash, and our immediate reaction was, *Please, Jesus, not again.* It was no consolation to those killed, but I think everyone breathed a sigh of relief when we discovered it was pilot error and not another terrorist act that brought flight 587 down.

CHAPTER 7

When a person is confronted with something overwhelmingly horrific there's a baseline for the stress, I later learned. Your senses are so awed by the enormity of the cataclysm, the sheer scope of the devastation, that you can't completely process the information that's assaulting your senses. Most people would probably just fall over at the sight of what we were confronted by, but we just blocked out the terror that crept in from all sides. Our only available remedy was to focus on our jobs. We were completely task oriented, and nothing large or small was permitted to distract us from fulfilling our responsibility.

What was even worse at Ground Zero than at most disasters, and the reminder would edge into your consciousness every time you saw a body, or a body part, was that there were thousands of people in that mountain of rubble.

Then there were those spikes of fear and anxiety that just sent your nervous system over the edge, such as every time you found a body part. But you had work to do, so you buried it, and eventually all that unreal devastation became the only reality in your life.

Everyone deals with stress, and as federal responders our only concern was doing our assignment to the best of our individual and collective abilities. All other considerations were secondary.

In that regard our mission was successfully completed: in all our time searching the site and its exiting truckloads of debris we never found any radioactive hot spots. The largest radiation signature we found in those four months was near the Fresh Kills landfill, where the debris was dumped, but the radiation was coming from an area not related to the WTC rubble, so it became secondary to our primary focus, which was Ground Zero.

I always wondered what had been put there, but it wasn't our responsibility to diagnose at the time.

Before we finished our task we had a helicopter from Andrews Air Force Base fly over with one of our large radiation scanners, just to verify that there were no hot spots at Ground Zero. There were none.

In the end, only two hundred eighty-nine bodies were found intact at the site. Nearly twenty thousand body parts were found. More than one thousand one hundred people were never identified, and more than one point five million tons of debris was removed from the area.

My team and I were there for the initial two weeks. I would have to stay for the next three and a half months.

CHAPTER 8

After four months working on the pile at Ground Zero, I was ordered by my superiors at DOE Headquarters to support a Nuclear Emergency Support Team (NEST), which had the responsibility of performing radiation searches throughout the northeast as well as conducting searches at various significant events throughout the region.

I hadn't had any time off since Sept. 11, but I didn't feel I needed it. Ground Zero had become my reality. Even though the transition didn't allow for any recuperative time, I was accustomed to this kind of schedule from my time in the U.S. Navy. You don't mind the pressure or physical exhaustion because you feel like you're contributing. You don't think about yourself, only how you can get your job accomplished and complete the overall objective.

We went to a family get-together with my wife's family once during that four month period, and the whole idea of sitting and talking to people without a care in the world was surreal. I felt more comfortable on the pile at Ground Zero. That nightmare had become my reality

But even though I was determined to keep working, and even though I felt fine, the schedule was, unbeknownst to me, laying a foundation for a horrible nightmare—a nightmare that would last the rest of my life.

My training in nuclear physics combined with what I learned in the navy qualified me to lead a NEST team. But, unlike most of the employees at Brookhaven Lab, I wasn't a government contractor; I was a federal agent. And DOE had the right to do with me as it pleased.

Most of my team had left Ground Zero long ago, as their presence there was largely voluntary and they had work to do back at Brookhaven Lab. I stayed, per my deployment orders by DOE, as part of the Crisis Management Team, coordinating with the other agencies on site; training NYPD officers on the use of radiation detectors (and they would subsequently train other officers, the NYPD being the size of a small army); and coordinating regular flyovers of Ground Zero and Fresh Kills Landfill, to reassure the New York City Department of Health that there were no dangerous radiation sources present.

Initially the NYPD officers were alarmed at how often the radiation detectors went off, but they quickly learned that many non-hazardous and legitimate items routinely gave off radioactive readings, including granite, radar and certain radio frequencies. The detectors went from being novelties to nuisances in no time.

Even though I wasn't prepared to join a NEST team, I wasn't unfamiliar with them. NEST teams weren't new, and as Regional Response Coordinator for DOE's Radiological Assistance Program (RAP), we'd done work similar to what NEST did in the past. Mostly our RAP teams were called to sites to measure radiation, identify the signature and report back.

Specific missions required a NEST response, but before 9/11 most of our responses were more often precautionary, such as industrial contamination or the disposal of medical equipment or isotopes.

Our RAP team at Brookhaven Lab did have several highly prolific cases. One high-profile case happened in June 1998. Investigators uncovered an apparent plot to assassinate several Long Island politicians with radioactive material in June of that year. Two men were arrested; the head conspirator, a fellow named John Ford, was a forty-seven-year-old former court officer and president of the Long Island UFO Network. Ford was taped soliciting people to use radium to poison Suffolk County Republican Party leader John Powell after an informant alerted the District Attorney's office.

Our RAP team was directed to a house in Bellport on Long Island, where Ford had stockpiled five canisters of radium, as well as handguns, ammunition, a mine detector, a gas mask and militia literature. It was certainly a unique and patient murder plot, with Ford apparently obsessed with hatred for mainstream political figures and hoping the eventual radium exposure would cause incurable diseases, and someday, death. Other politicians targeted included two other Republican county officials, legislator Fred Towle and Brookhaven public safety director Anthony Gazzola.

I was later requested to testify for the state against Ford before the Grand Jury, after which he was found mentally unfit to stand trial. To this day Ford's supporters insist that his arrest on attempted murder charges was a frame-up by the federal government, determined to prevent his investigation into the United States' cover-up of UFO landings.

A more typical scenario, pre-9/11, occurred when we were contacted by Pennsylvania's director of the Office of Emergency Management (OEM), an old friend of mine named Bill Dornsife. They wanted my team to investigate a metal shredding plant in Reading, where sensors had detected radiation coming from a truck loaded with "auto-fluff," or non-metal debris left over after the auto shredding process.

We reached the plant in Reading in the morning and were greeted by a plant official, who we later learned was actually a consultant, giving us a lot of grief and telling us our services weren't needed, that the state and the NRC had both said the plant was safe. Such responses weren't surprising, because businesses *really* don't want their work interfered with, and certainly not something that could make the public panicky. When word gets out that there's radioactive contamination at a facility, it casts the business in a bad light, and the location of this plant was in a residential area and was already an unpopular topic. The NRC and the state teams had identified the source as Americium by the signature that the isotope gave off. Each isotope has a distinct signature, kind of like a fingerprint. The signature comes in the form of different levels of energy. By looking at the different energies coming from a radioactive source, physicists can tell which isotope they are dealing with. This is a big factor when you are dealing with malevolent uses of radioactive material, or RAM. Only certain isotopes can be used to produce an atomic or nuclear bomb and those materials are extremely heavily guarded by security forces, some with the authority to kill if they believe that the safety or security of a U.S. owned nuclear device or material is being compromised. But that is a whole different story in itself.

Anyway, I called Bill, who told me to put the "plant official" on the phone. I could faintly hear a lot of screaming coming from the other side of the phone line and the consultant just kept repeating, "Yes sir, yes sir, yes sir." Within minutes we were welcomed into the plant.

It did not take us long at all to ascertain that the plant was not clean at all. The Americium was everywhere, and there was no way to separate the minute particles of radioactive material from the auto fluff it was mixed with. After spending two days on what was supposed to be an afternoon deployment we realized that this was turning into a remediation project, so we called EPA, who sent in remediation contractors to clean up the contaminated materials and dispose of them. We did arrange for shipment of the larger chunks of RAM that the state and NRC teams had located and placed in a lead shield. We re-packaged the Ram properly and arranged to have it shipped to another DOE lab in New Mexico.

We later heard that DOE's lab in Albuquerque was able to identify the source number and tracked the Americium source back to Strohs Brewing Company's Latrobe, PA, plant, where they apparently used it in a device that gauged the thickness of the aluminum in their beer cans. How it was ever accidentally discarded with other scrap metal is a mystery, but it was typical of the calls the RAP team was sent out on.

Another typical scenario would be a call from a municipal health department who had just received a radiation alarm on one of the city's garbage truck pulling into a transfer point. The truck was placed over in a vacant corner and we would be called in to examine the situation. After several hours of conducting radiation surveys and digging through the garbage we would find the culprit. An adult dirty diaper containing feces from someone who had undergone a radiation treatment of some sort and improperly disposed of their diapers. Oh what fun those missions were.

CHAPTER 9

Jumping onto a NEST team from a RAP team required some additional training on the conduct of deployment operations and the equipment being used; unfortunately, the existing NEST team was reluctant to provide that training to me or my team, and initially we were treated like luggage, carried along for the ride whenever the team was called out on assignment.

Before 9/11, NEST teams were assigned to specific tasks, but in the wake of 9/11 radiation became a twenty-four/seven interest of the federal government. What if terrorists snuck a nuclear weapon into the country? Where had the near-mythical Soviet "suitcase nukes" (so small they could be carried in a suitcase) gone after the empire's dissolution? What if terrorists had access to depleted isotopes and were planning on detonating a "dirty bomb" in a heavily populated area? ("Dirty bombs," which the public heard a great deal about in the aftermath of 9/11, are conventional weapons with radioactive isotopes attached; they only destroy what the conventional weapon destroys, but the strewn radioactive material leaves quite a mess).

And the administration was unhappy that the NEST teams were only activated from Albuquerque, New Mexico and Las Vegas, Nevada. They wanted teams that could respond more quickly to every area of the country. So the program was expanded into eight regional teams, built out of existing RAP teams, and one such team was assigned to cover the Northeast, Region One.

Some background on the NEST program is essential: NEST was formed in 1975 after a Boston man threatened to detonate a nuclear device unless he was given $200,000. It was a hoax, as were all subsequent threats, but the team was deployed several times annually through the mid-1990s to investigate potential nuclear incidents.

NEST works under the National Nuclear Security Administration (NNSA), preparing and equipping specialized response teams to deal with the technical aspects of nuclear or radiological terrorism. NEST capabilities include search and identification of nuclear materials, diagnostics and assessment of suspected nuclear devices, processing of the material or device, and packaging for the transport of materials.

NEST members include engineers, scientists, and other technical specialists from NNSA's nuclear weapons laboratories and facilities to include Los Alamos National Laboratory in New Mexico, where the atomic bomb was developed in the 1940s; Sandia National Laboratories, which is owned by Lockheed Martin; Lawrence Livermore National Laboratory, which is operated by the University of California and dedicated to weapons research; and the Pantex Plant in Texas, where weapons are assembled and disassembled.

NEST teams are also accompanied by firepower, sometimes a great deal of firepower. In my team's case, it was usually provided by Special Ops forces from another supporting federal agency, and while all the weapons were intended to make us feel more secure, it had precisely the opposite effect.

We would often walk into a scenario which included the possibility of terrorists determined to detonate a device and carrying weapons, and we would be surrounded by agents armed with semi-automatic weapons and wearing body armor, while we were wearing nothing protective and carrying radiation sensors. If terrorists were armed and decided to start shooting, we would be in the crossfire with no protection. And if it were me trying to use a device in a malevolent manner, I'd probably want to shoot the guy who can detect it.

I was reluctant to carry weapons or have my team members armed not only because it was a bad idea (most of my team members where scientists/physicists and as such were high-strung to begin with), but also we weren't trained on the weapons or authorized to carry them, despite some agents' attempts to arm us. If a NEST team member accidentally shot a civilian, or even a soldier or federal agent, it would be both tragic and viewed as an enormous mistake on my part, whether or not I allowed it. It would have generated such a media blitz with yours truly as the "flavor of the week."

One time during an operation, an agent stopped the special search vehicle we were riding in so he could go into a local restaurant and use the bathroom. He pulled a 9 mm Glock pistol and handed it to me. I looked at it in disbelief and asked him where the safety was on the gun.

"It doesn't have one," he replied.

So I handed it back. "You can keep it," I said.

NEST agents have no authority to arrest or kill anyone. We'd make good targets, though, and we'd make excellent scapegoats if an assignment went awry and civilians were killed. I could see myself sitting in front of Congress, explaining why, with no authority or training to use firepower, a member of my team had accidentally killed a civilian, and spending the next few years in jail as someone's regular date because I hadn't used proper precaution. The thought made me nauseous, as I am allergic to makeup and lipstick.

I have no fear of guns, per se, or moral reservations about them. I was a hunter from the time I was very young, but carrying a Glock 9 mm semi-automatic with no safety into a potentially volatile situation with members of the general public in attendance was a whole different situation.

We were repeatedly told that we would be getting body armor from our superiors in D.C., along with a laundry list of equipment that would have made us safer and more productive, but we were never accommodated. Given what the Special Ops guys were carrying, body armor would have been reassuring.

CHAPTER 10

In addition to NEST teams, the government began deploying radiation detectors at ports at home and abroad, in an attempt to short-circuit any attempt to send weapons or dirty bomb components across America's borders.

In essence, with the deployment of radiation detectors and trained personnel at key points of entry, the United States was beginning a bold, and some might say virtually impossible, attempt to create a radiation detection shield around the country to ward off a clandestine nuclear attack. It was similar to the protection we'd had with NORAD (North American Aerospace Defense Command) since the Cold War to warn us of overt nuclear attacks, though the guiding principle of our radar system was mutually assured destruction of the enemy, not prevention of nuclear war.

This idea, in contrast, would ring the mainland United States with radiation detectors and connect these sensors to military and police command centers, which would then respond or activate local teams, NEST and other federal responders to any detected radioactive materials.

The logic of the plan is obvious; the plan's inherent flaw is the massive logistical requirement of screening thousands of miles of mostly unguarded borders with expensive radiation detection equipment, much of which had yet to be manufactured, operated by personnel who had yet to be trained, with many areas of our borders unguarded and impossible to monitor.

And I'd worked around radiation long enough to know that, even with strict vigilance, determined terrorists would still have the capacity to smuggle radioactive materials into the country. As massive as those container ships are that dock at American ports every day, there'd be no way to detect a radioactive isotope in a lead-lined box.

An understanding just what radiation can do is helpful to understanding what makes NEST, and other surveillance and preventive operations, critical. Everyone understands that nuclear weapons are dangerous and frightening, but the immediate effect of an atomic blast which vaporizes everything in the immediate area is preferable, to those in the know, over radiation poisoning.

A brief radiation exposure can result in acute radiation syndrome; chronic radiation syndrome requires a prolonged high level of exposure. Radiation sickness is generally associated with acute exposure and has characteristic symptoms, such as nausea and fatigue, which appear in an orderly fashion. The symptoms of radiation sickness become more serious (and the chance of survival decreases) as the dosage of radiation increases.

Longer term exposure to radiation, as witnessed in Japan and around the Chernobyl site in Russia, can induce cancer as genes are mutated, and cause birth defects in subsequent children. Potassium iodide, administered orally immediately after radiation exposure, is used to protect the thyroid from absorbing radioactive iodine in the event of an accident or terrorist attack at a nuclear power plant, or the detonation of a weapon, but potassium iodide isn't effective against a dirty bomb unless it contains radioactive iodine, and even then it would only help to prevent thyroid cancer.

Because the hysteria that generally accompanies fear of radioactive contamination, the public wasn't informed about the deployment of NEST teams and radiation screeners, and they were never aware that radiation detection was going on all around them. Our presence was off the radar, even to the average cop on the beat, which wasn't always easy.

We were dressed as civilians, wearing normal street clothes that allowed us to blend into whatever environment we were operating in. We carried small gamma and neutron detectors that were disguised in different ways, so we were never conspicuous in public.

Equipped in this way, my team was able to wander the streets in public at any time, and even through heavily populated events like the Democratic National Convention in Boston, the World Series, the Republican National Convention in New York City, and the U.S. Open in Queens. We also scanned the United Nations any time it was in full session, Madison Square Garden for sporting events, subways, train stations, and the President's hotel any time he visited a city in our region.

In addition to the NEST teams, which are in constant motion, it has been estimated that since 9/11 our government has distributed more than fifteen hundred radiation detectors to overseas ports and border crossings, as well as to America's Mexican and Canadian borders, domestic seaports, Coast Guard ships, airports, railways, and mail facilities, with additional detectors being distributed as fast as they can be built and personnel can be trained to operate them.

I hope the radiation detection personnel are trained better and are more logical in their thought processes than the screeners at airports, who forced me to hand over two and a half fluid ounces of hand sanitizer, only to watch them toss this alleged potential biohazard or explosive into the garbage can next to their screening station. In a real HazMat world that would NEVER have happened. If we took something from someone because we felt it was potentially dangerous, we had to treat it as if it were, not toss it into a garbage can, especially one sitting right there at the choke point created by the security process.

But even with this growing arsenal of detectors, America's borders are too open to catch everything. Crossing the border with weapons is no more challenging than crossing as an illegal alien, and as we've discovered in recent years, there's no stopping a determined illegal alien any more than it's possible to stop someone determined to do us harm.

Then there's the Homeland Security funding, which has been rightly called politically skewed and illogical. States that are truly vulnerable like New York and New Jersey have received far less money per capita than states like Wyoming and South Dakota. New Jersey can list Port Elizabeth as a site, and the rest of the country just shrugs, but more cargo flows through Port Elizabeth than any other port in the United States. South Dakota lists Mount Rushmore, and everyone nods knowingly: of course, it's a national landmark. You have to protect that.

But terrorists aren't going to risk their lives getting a weapon into the country, or building a weapon here so they can use it to blow up a rock. You look at some of the sites being protected, and wonder at the logic. The Grand Canyon? Will they make the hole bigger? The Painted Desert? Who would smuggle in a nuke in order to blow up a sandbox? Homeland Security funding is an example of pork barrel politics at its worst, because it doesn't only waste money, it endangers lives. Politicians trying to pretend that they know what they are doing by directing field elements to do asinine things—such is the situation in the Middle East with Iraq and Afghanistan. Leave the military fighting to the generals and butt your dumb ivy-league-school-graduated noses out of it. If you want to control what's going on then sign up, put on a uniform and get your ass over there. Hump around that hot desert for a few months, and if you live, then come back and tell the public your views. I cannot stand it when politicians puts on airs of reverence that, quite frankly, they haven't earned. Okay, so you won a popularity contest, you didn't get there by having foresight or reverence, you just had more money or more "dirt" on the other guy.

The world is filled with so many uncontrolled and transportable radioactive materials that building a dirty bomb wouldn't be difficult. Most of the radioactive materials in question are harmless, but many detectors are too primitive to distinguish between different types of radiation, and they ring just as loudly if they locate nuclear-bomb material or granite or, for that matter, bananas, which emit radiation from the isotope potassium-40. Even people who have recently received medical treatments with radioactive isotopes such as thorium can set off the detectors.

It was reported that at the baseball All-Star Game in Detroit in 2005, NEST team members screened thousands of fans entering the stadium, and their sensors rang just once, when they scanned former

Secretary of Energy Spencer Abraham, who was emitting radiation from a recent doctor's visit.

We had a similar experience at the Democratic Convention in Boston, when a newspaper columnist undergoing radiation therapy set off our scanners. He was given a pass for the remainder of the convention, but we asked him if he wouldn't mind passing through each of our scanners every day so we could calibrate the devices. He was tickled to be an insider in the process, and even wrote about it in his column.

None of the radioactive materials detected by NEST teams so far, at least as has been publicly acknowledged, would be useful to a terrorist seeking to build a nuclear weapon, but some of it might be useful for a dirty bomb, and it's likely that terrorists would be more inclined to pursue a dirty bomb, based on the easier availability of its components.

CHAPTER 11

Of course, doing our work off the public's radar did occasionally create problems.

New York City was an obvious problem area for me and my team members, because we'd trained many emergency workers in the city over the years, and I was nearly spotted by people I knew while on patrol. Secrecy was mandated, so even friends, relatives and colleagues weren't allowed to know our mission, and anyone who would recognize me would also know that my responsibility, whether RAP or NEST, involved testing for radiation. By connecting such dots an incident might ensue, which would complicate our mission and unnecessarily worry the public.

Then there were the police, who were more alert to anomalies or suspicious behavior after 9/11. And since we were frequently working in major metropolitan areas, our vehicles were often struck by—or themselves struck—other vehicles, which required us to reach out to our contacts within local law enforcement, who would then send over a special unit to sort out the problem.

Early one morning around five or six a.m., my escort and I were heading downtown in Manhattan to sweep around the New York Stock Exchange when we came to a police roadblock. Our vehicle was waved through, and then through a second one, but at the third roadblock a police sergeant approached the vehicle. He was dressed in black, as were his officers; it was a Hercules Team, an NYPD special events squad. The sergeant looked at our vehicle and was getting suspicious.

"You've got old New York plates," he observed. "And you've got no inspection sticker." We also had no vehicle registration. "Get out of the vehicle," he ordered.

My escort explained that we weren't permitted to leave our vehicle. We didn't explain our reason to him, but we had radiation sensors in the back and couldn't allow anyone to search the vehicle.

"Do you have any credentials?" asked the sergeant.

We had never needed them before this. We retrieved what we had in our wallets.

"You work for the federal government?" asked the sergeant. "You'd think they'd give you something better than these cheesy looking credentials." I thought, *Yeah, if the federal government didn't have to give out so much money to you state and local guys we probably could afford better looking "creds," and equipment, too!*

They brought out a bomb dog, and I could hear someone trying to open the back of the vehicle. When I tried to get out of the passenger's side door, I was immediately grabbed by a cop and could feel a gun barrel pressed against my nose. "Don't move," the cop said.

We sat there being stared down by fifteen to twenty cops carrying machine guns until eight a.m., when we were finally able to reach our contact, an NYPD deputy commissioner who got us past the roadblock.

We scanned the Stock Exchange and left, on to our next assignment.

Whenever we set up a Tactical Operation Center (TOC) we tried to pick a spot where we had plenty of enclosed garage space for working on our vehicles and configuring our equipment in the vehicles while staying undetected. We would also try to ensure that the space was in an obscure location. Most of the time this would happen in a "client" controlled parking garage or facility, and these places tended to be damp, dirty and nasty places, hot in the summer, cold in the winter and usually located in really bad neighborhoods.

As a result we sometimes had problems with our neighbors.

There were hookers in the neighborhood who regularly serviced their customers in front of our metal rollup door. We were supposed to look inconspicuous, and we were, because to the locals we were just another building. Another time a drug deal went bad down the block, and from the safety of our cave we heard the gunshots.

Then there was the guy who decided to piss on the side metal roll-up door one night. A lot of homeless people slept in front of the building because there was scaffolding overhead that provided shelter from the elements. I heard what sounded like water running down the exterior of the door, so I banged on it and yelled. If that guy only knew what was on the other side of that ordinary looking door: guns, ammo, radiation detectors and federal agents.

Another time we heard a van pull up, followed by the sound of someone working the padlock. He was determined to steal whatever was behind that metal door, no matter what it was. I obviously couldn't let him do that, so I started yelling and he took off.

The odd thing was, photographers seemed to like that the neighborhood was so "colorful," so they'd set up photo shoots with half-naked models on the sidewalk. Maybe having a beautiful woman posing in a slum somehow makes her look that much more attractive.

CHAPTER 12

After three months working with us, the members of the original Las Vegas NEST team returned home. With one day's notice we were ordered to take over operations in May of 2002.

I was in a Compartmentalized Special Information (CSI) meeting in Washington, DC, with my counterparts from across the DOE complex. It was a brainstorming session to discuss the future of the NEST team and search missions. CSI is a special classification that has additional security criteria above that of Top Secret. The government breaks its nuclear weapons program into twelve different areas, or sigmas, so that no one person has clearance in every area of the program. I had clearance in eight sigmas, or so I was told— nobody really knew for sure (I guess that information was classified). I was granted the sigmas in order to have access to information in the event we detected a nuclear weapon radioactive signature.

The CSI meetings, which were attended by the leaders of each of the NEST teams, were an opportunity to receive limited diagnostic and analytical updates and to receive information from our superiors.

Or, in the case of the Las Vegas NEST team, their manager wanted to get his guys pulled off the current on-going mission.

"The Vegas guys want to stand down," I was told by my superior. "You're going to have to pick this up, and you can't turn it down."

"That's a problem," I replied. "We haven't actually been trained on most of this equipment."

I began to get an uneasy feeling in the pit of my stomach as though someone had just sucker-punched me, and I just realized it. I felt as though the Vegas team wanted us to fail, to show headquarters and the rest of the complex that only they could do this type of work, not a bunch of RAP team incompetents.

This revised assignment was very complicated and daunting, as the original NEST team members had been so proprietary about their equipment we were mostly in the dark about how to operate and maintain it. They had radiological detection equipment of assorted sizes, some so big it had to be transported on a plane while others were so small they could fit in a briefcase, and the crew I'd brought with me from DOE had little experience with most of it.

We'd spent three months with these guys, and they'd mostly and deliberately kept us in the dark.

It was typical of many of the decisions that came out of Washington, which were sometimes personal or political rather than logical. The feds weren't concerned with the practical applications of their decisions; how to actually do the job was left to those of us assigned the task. And because he could get away with it, the Vegas Project Manager was willing to leave us, and logically, the northeastern United States, unprepared.

Another example of bureaucracy run amuck was when someone influential sent a letter to a DOE official outlining the scenario of a nuclear weapon being smuggled through Port Elizabeth in a container, and suggested that we scan all the containers at the port as a precaution.

A container, for those unaware, is what's pulled behind an eighteen-wheeler, and the cargo ships carry dozens of them at a time, stacked together like building blocks. Scanning every container at Port Elizabeth would have been an infinite job for our team, with no rest, ever, and even then we would never have had the time to scan everything. Fortunately, logic prevailed in that situation, and we were never given the assignment.

Anyone can sit around hypothesizing about what might be done, or what might happen. That takes no insight or energy, not like actually addressing real problems as they arise.

So we received a half-day training from one of the outgoing Las Vegas NEST agents, then went out in the field uncomfortably shouldering the responsibility left to us. Eventually we learned how to work all the equipment and built our own training program, so that every team member had backup on every piece of equipment.

Last I heard, DOE still uses the equipment training program we developed with its new NEST agents, so our effort went to good use beyond our immediate needs.

CHAPTER 13

One of our biggest and most public NEST cases involved a cargo ship docked in Port Elizabeth.

It was the morning of Sept. 10, 2002 and POTUS was coming to New York City the following day for the one year anniversary of the terrorist attacks to address the workers at Ground Zero. POTUS is an acronym we used for President Of The United States. The fact that POTUS was coming to our region always created a heightened sense of urgency.

During the couple of weeks prior to this we had been assisting the Coast Guard boarding parties with searching for potential RAM smuggling. I don't want to digress too much here, but one thing I wanted to point out is how both the Navy and the Coast Guard had all these "parties." There were stores-handling parties, weapons-loading parties and boarding parties. Funny thing was, I don't remember them being much of a party and they sure as heck were not any fun. Anyway…

The Coast Guard has a database program, based in Washington, DC, that tracks vessels of interest all over the world. They know who owns them, what ports they've visited, and whether they've been scanned for radiation at any point in their journey. Any number of things can trigger red flags on a transport vessel, and once that ship has been identified as a High Interest Vessel (HIV), and it's coming to an American port, all pertinent security is notified, including a NEST search team.

The M/V Palermo Senator, a seven hundred eight-foot container ship owned by a German subsidiary of South Korea-based Hanjin, shipping and sailing under Liberian registry, was flagged as an HIV that week. The ship had stopped in Singapore, Malaysia and Egypt, among other destinations, but the red flag was likely raised over its stop at the Italian hub port of Gioia Tauro on August 25. The port, on the southern Italian coast, was a suspicious site because small container ships from the Black Sea, Mediterranean, Middle East, North Africa and Italy use the port, and it is suspected of being a preferred transit point for al Qaeda members seeking to transport materials.

In fact, in October, 2001, a forty-three-year-old Egyptian named Rigk Amid Farid had been caught at Gioia Touro port aboard the German ship Ipex Emperor, hidden in a container which had been converted into a living quarters, including furniture, cell phones and enough food, water and batteries for three weeks, and Canadian passports and entry permits for security personnel and mechanics at Kennedy, Newark and O'Hare airports.

An investigation showed the container had been loaded at Egypt's Port Said and painted over to disguise it as the property of the giant Danish Maersk Sealand container company, which it replaced. But an Italian court ordered Farid released on bail, upon which he disappeared.

The Palermo Senator was moored at Port Elizabeth, New Jersey. The Coast Guard identified her as an HIV and requested our help. My team arrived at the Senator's mooring and met with members of the Coast Guard's boarding party. I asked the boarding party leader why this ship had been identified as an HIV that required us to search for a nuclear device. He responded that a previous boarding party from the day before heard a noise coming from one of the containers on board. A Coast Guardsman thought he heard a noise coming from the hold. It was entirely possible that there was human cargo, because sometimes people would stow away, and there was always the possibility that al Qaeda would try to sneak operatives into the country aboard a container ship. Somehow someone suggested that the noise might be a nuclear warhead.

"Nukes only make one noise," I said. "And you don't get to hear it for very long."

It had always been my contention that if you look long enough and hard enough for something, you'll probably find it. The question was: What do you do when you find it. What that something was, wasn't clear. We were getting a radiation signature, but the containers were stacked in the enormous hold, and there was no way of knowing what the signature indicated without looking inside the container. The metal containers and their contents were "scattering" the radiation signals all over the place. Each member of my five-man team took a turn with the sensor, and each of us got the same reading. By researching the ships Dangerous Cargo Manifest we were able to determine that she should not have been carrying anything with RAM onboard. Red flags went up.

What had begun as an anomaly had become a pattern. I notified DOE headquarters of what we had found. They ordered us to send the data through the appropriate channels to have it analyzed by the weapons experts, which we did. I did know that weapon designers and nuclear physicists available to interpret our readings so they could make informed estimates of what we were looking at. We had quadruple-verified the spot on the vessel and the radioactive signature, but we couldn't identify the isotope. There was too much shielding by the container and scattering of the signature. Metals and other materials interact with and affect gamma rays.

We waited a while and then got the callback that the experts needed better data and we should gather a longer time-shot of information. We again did as we were told. By now word had gotten out by the shipyard workers that something was going on with the Senator and that plainclothes federal agents were scurrying all around the place. By this time the FBI, US Coast Guard, US Customs, Newark Police Department, NJ State Police and Defense Intelligence Agency all had personnel on the scene.

Soon the news crews arrived at the dock, as did the protesters. I'm still not sure what they were protesting; I didn't have time to ask.

We could see news helicopters flying overhead trying to get a shot of what was going on.

It was getting late in the day and the call came back to take a longer shot of the source, at which, again, we complied with head-quarters' orders.

"Get everybody off the ship!" somebody ordered. "Confiscate their cell phones! They could detonate a bomb with a cell phone!" *We don't know that there's a bomb on board*, I thought. But fear had taken control, and the entire place was on the verge of hysteria.

So they began to evacuate the ship and remove everyone to a secure location. This task was performed by the Coast Guard's Sea Marshals, some BIG dudes that you did not want to mess with.

The crew, most of which didn't appear to speak English, was sequestered, as were the passengers. Passage on a container ship may not be glamorous, but apparently it's an economical way to see the world.

The next logical step at this point would have been to lift the container in question from the hold with a crane, open it up and examine its contents. That, however, is not what happened next. What happened next was an accumulation of information on the Palermo Senator that added to our list of potential circumstances, but didn't clarify the container's contents.

Everybody and his brother claimed to have insider information on the ship: the owner is friends with Saddam Hussein and smuggles munitions to him, the ship has been known to transport nuclear fuel, and on and on. It was like sharks at a feeding frenzy. You could feel the excitement bursting through the roof.

While we waited for a decision, I directed my team into the hold and took another reading, and got the same results.

The parent company, Hanjin, asked to have their containers offloaded. This, of course, aroused additional suspicion.

I had no idea we're at war with South Korea, I thought.

Finally, as we approached ten p.m., headquarters gave me permission to remove the containers and examine them on the dock.

A huge boom crane moved into position. The crane operator asked that a NEST team member stand next to him, to alert him if the radiation was at a dangerous level. DOE Headquarters ordered us to stay back two hundred feet in case there was an explosion.

Why, so I can see the flash before I'm vaporized? I thought.

As the crane operator was moving into place I found myself in a room with the head of the Newark FBI Office and the USCG Captain of the Port for New York City. We were discussing possible actions and ramifications when they both looked at me and the FBI agent asked me, "Do we tell POTUS not to come?"

I can not describe the feeling that welled up inside me at that moment, knowing I was making a decision concerning the security and safety of the most powerful man on Earth. The tension was so thick you could cut it with a knife. Me, a lowly country boy from Havelock, N.C., holding the safety of the President in my hands—I think I felt my heart stop, I know my breathing had.

I finally said I needed to call Washington. Then the captain took charge and said he was in command and ordered the ship to sea. We canceled the offloading and moved the ship eight miles offshore to Ambrose Anchorage. POTUS was just twelve hours away, and the Captain of the Port wasn't going to be held responsible for getting the President nuked.

My NEST team was ordered to stand down, and I was relieved. It had been a circus, poorly managed and highly publicized, and I wanted no further part of it.

The crew had the Palermo Senator off the dock in less than half an hour. They were probably relieved to be free of their sequestering.

A Coast Guard ship took out a NEST relief team, along with enough firepower to start a war, to secure the ship at sea. *If it really is a nuclear weapon, what good are guns?* I thought. But my opinion didn't matter at that point, if it ever had.

They also had to send out a floating crane, a crew, and spent millions of dollars to do what we should have been authorized to do all along: offload the container in question at the dock.

The relief NEST team found that containers in Bay Forty-two showed high gamma signals with no presence of neutrons, revealing the presence of K-40, and Uranium and Thorium daughters. The source: ceramic tiles and marble. Apparently, a lot of the soil in Eastern Europe has a radioactive signature from the fallout from the Chernobyl reactor's meltdown, and these tiles were made in that region, though no one was ever certain precisely what caused the signature.

CHAPTER 14

Afterward, I met with my superiors in Washington to discuss my team's role in the investigation. "What instruments were you guys using to get those readings?" I was asked.

"The instruments you provided us with for the job," I replied.

"How much training have you had on these instruments?"

"As much training as you provided us before the Las Vegas NEST team stood down in May," I answered.

"We spent a lot of money on this trying to determine if there was a nuclear bomb on board," I was reminded.

"I never said it was a bomb," I said. "I said we found a radiation signature."

I reminded them that we had the option of removing the hatch and offloading the container, and we would have known by five p.m. that it was tile and marble. But no one who was authorized to make a decision would make a decision.

It was clearly a black mark against me and my team, but they declined to penalize us. Instead, after clearly implying that we were unqualified and poorly equipped, they took the next illogical step: they increased our workload.

Headquarters was certainly never at fault. I learned that about Washington long ago: no one there will ever take a hit as long as there's someone lower who can take the blame. It reminded me of a saying they had in the service, "Shit rolls downhill." If you're on the bottom you get all the crap.

A few days later we were tasked to support the Coast Guard again with a ship that was offshore at Ambrose Anchor Station, where container ships awaited their turn to unload. The NEST team left at six a.m. from the Sandy Hook station onboard a 47-foot Coastie boat. The boarding party consisted of my NEST team, a bomb squad, including a bomb-sniffing dog, a U.S. Customs official and a Coast Guard boarding/inspection team.

A 47-foot boat doesn't quite match up with a 708-foot container vessel, so in order to board her the Coastie skipper drew the 47's bow as close as possible, at which time we were expected to grab onto a rope that had been lowered and pull ourselves aboard. We had to stand on the bow and wait for the ocean's swell to boost us higher against the ship's side. It's a difficult but logical maneuver, unless you're a bomb-sniffing dog lacking opposable thumbs, in which case you have to be caged and hauled aboard on a rope. I can still see that poor dog's cage being hauled through the air, a stream of urine pouring from it as it rose.

Having just gone through the Palermo Senator ordeal, I was not anxious for a repeat, so unless our radiation detectors were able to reach up, grab me by the collar and slap my face while yelling, "It's a bomb!" I wasn't going to call anyone or report anything.

On some of the missions we were on I had no idea who I was speaking to when I called Washington, just disembodied voices. I was fairly certain that they were in the War Room, and I had heard rumors that Vice President Cheney took a lot of interest in NEST team activities, but I never knew for certain who I was taking my orders from. *Mine is not to question why, mine is but to do or die, hoorah.*"

CHAPTER 15

I felt like a monkey in the middle at DOE. Compounding the problem was that I had a dual alliance of command. Brookhaven Lab was in charge of my personnel orders, and Washington provided my operating orders. But I wasn't permitted to tell all my superiors at Brookhaven what my team's activities were, because they might not have the security clearance to be given such information.

They couldn't have screwed up the process worse if they tried.

When I pointed out the unnecessary complication of the arrangement, management worked out a Memorandum of Understanding, which stated that Brookhaven would provide administrative support to the NEST team. Other than timekeeping, they didn't, of course, and whenever they did, they expected me to pay for it out of my operational budget.

You can't squeeze blood from a stone, I repeatedly told them, and if you could, what makes you think I have it? But the status quo never improved.

My health, on the other hand, gave an inkling of what was to come the summer of 2005.

I developed a cough; in retrospect, the first sign that working on the pile might have affected my health. It was during the NEST team's detail at the Republican National Convention, and it wasn't just a cough; it was the worst cough I've ever had. I coughed so hard I burst a blood vessel, and the whole side of my chest turned purple, and there was a raised lump.

My doctor sent me for a mammogram, just to make sure it wasn't cancer. The procedure gave me greater sympathy for what women go through. That was *painful.*

The technician was pushing me forward and clamping down on my chest, and finally I said, "You know, I can't be more than an A-cup here. That's as much as you're going to get."

On the bright side, since 9/11, I had remarried. The Palermo Senator investigation reminded me that I was vulnerable. Our task as a RAP team had been primarily accident containment; with NEST it was ostensibly counter-terrorism. And here I was, in my forties, jumping aboard cargo ships that might contain bombs or terrorists, or terrorists with bombs, and I had a child at home and no one to look after him or my affairs if something happened to me.

I'm too old to be jumping boat to boat, I thought.

I'd met Sue, my wife, in December, 1999 at a Christmas party for Brookhaven employees. I was talking with a buddy when several women walked by, and I commented, "I kind of like that hen at the end." So I went over to her and began talking, and offered to buy her a drink.

"It's an open bar," she said.

We hit it off right away, and we married in secret on Nov. 23, 2002, a little more than two months after the Palermo Senator investigation. I'd had a gun in my face by then and I had another big deployment coming up. I wasn't feeling my best, not sick yet, just uneasy. I am not fatalistic, just a realist.

A retired town judge whom I'm friends with married us in our home in Flanders, Long Island, on the Saturday after Thanksgiving. Her parents were there as best man and woman, and my youngest son served as our only witness.

Later we decided to have a formal church wedding, so on July 5, 2003, we were married in the United Methodist Church in Riverhead, Long Island, New York. Notice how whenever you mention a town on Long Island people always say "Whereverville, Looong Island, New York." That's because there is something different and special about this piece of real estate.

CHAPTER 16

I always liked science, which is what led to my career in nuclear studies and in a long and roundabout fashion to my presence at Ground Zero.

My father was a career military man who had served in World War II, Korea and Vietnam, but it was my stepfather, another Marine who served in Vietnam, who, along with my mother, raised me.

I grew up in Havelock, North Carolina, in Craven County, a small southern town that would be indistinguishable from most other towns except for the Cherry Point Marine Corps Air Station, which made Havelock a convenient place for military families to live.

Originally named Havelock Station in the 1850s when the Atlantic and North Carolina Railroad built a depot there, the town was the landing point for the Battle of New Bern during the Civil War, when Union Gen. Ambrose Burnside (for whom sideburns are named) embarked from Roanoke Island to rendezvous with Union gunboats at Hatteras Inlet for an expedition. The Rhode Island Heavy artillery came ashore near the location of the current Officer's Club on Cherry Point Marine Corps Air Station and also near the Carolina Pines Golf and Country Club. Union forces captured nine forts and forty-one heavy guns and occupied a base, and despite subsequent Confederate assaults didn't leave until after the end of the war.

And some of the old-timers in town had a collective memory of the Union occupation; to them, the Civil War was still being fought, and Yankees weren't to be trusted.

Money was tight after my Dad bought our house. My mother didn't work, as most women didn't in those days, but he had trouble keeping up with the bills, so he began working evenings for a Mr. Oglesby, a fellow former Marine who operated a heating and air conditioning business. That's how I spent most of my spare time when I was growing up, working with my Dad in the heating and air conditioning business, and when he lost his driver's license I drove him everywhere.

Shortly after I had joined the service I stopped by the Oglesby's, probably to pick something up for my father, and Mrs. Oglesby remarked that she'd heard I had enlisted. "You don't trust them damn Yankees," she warned me.

I didn't say anything. You didn't back talk senior citizens in those days, or you'd get a whipping from your folks for your disrespectful attitude.

On weekends I would help Dad cut firewood, or rather, he would drink beer and watch me while I cut firewood. We'd sometimes spend the better part of the weekend at it, and we'd sell the wood for $20 a cord. He gave me $5 and kept the rest, so one day I asked him why he got to keep most of the money.

"My truck, my gas, my chainsaw," he replied. It was similar when we bought a boat together: he said my portion of the money paid for the steering wheel, so it was my job to drive. I didn't answer back when he treated me this way (which was all the time), but I was definitely anxious to get out of Havelock the first opportunity I saw.

It wasn't all work, though. We fished all the time, surf casting when I was younger and eventually graduating to a sixteen-foot Harker's Island boat. Harker's Island is an interesting place near Havelock; Ebenezer Harker purchased the island in 1730, settled there with his family, and built a plantation and boat yard, and the residents there are famous for their boats. The kids from the island I went to school with had to take a boat; there's still no other way to get on or off. It's said that some Harkers Island residents speak a distinct dialect of English after being separated from the mainland for so long.

We mostly caught bluefish for bait to catch Spanish and King mackerel. One time we went on a charter boat with a bunch of other Marines and not only caught our limit, we pulled in so many fifty-pound king mackerel that the freezer was filled and we had to return after only four hours out.

My Dad had converted an old refrigerator into a freezer and put it on my aunt's back porch, so he put all our king mackerel in there. Shortly after, I was camping in the nearby woods with some friends, and someone had brought a bottle of Boone's Farm wine, and we were passing it around, getting toasty, and someone said, "Hey, I know where we can get something to eat."

I knew what was coming, and sure enough we snuck onto my aunt's back porch and swiped a king mackerel from the freezer. We ran back to our campsite and set it to cook over our bonfire pit, but being kids we forgot about it and only remembered when it was burned on one side and sushi on the other. We had to toss the fish, but it was basically harmless fun.

I also hunted a lot. We lived in Croatan National Forest, so there was plenty of game, though we usually hunted squirrels and rabbits. We were sitting on tree stumps in the forest one time, and my Dad was making squirrel "chirps," trying to entice the squirrels to come investigate.

In the distance came the sound of something crashing through the brush. It was a man, dressed in buckskin like Daniel Boone with not a speck of orange on him, carrying an enormous gun, stomping around like he owned the forest.

"I'd better stop or this guy'll shoot us," Dad whispered.

The hunter was oblivious. He walked within fifty feet of us, came to a fence and tossed his gun over before climbing over. My Dad would've beat my ass if I had done that; you never toss a gun because it could go off. You set it gently on the other side of the fence, but some people think the rules don't apply to them. Not wearing orange was a clear sign that he hadn't thought hunting through very carefully.

When you live in a remote area you can take *some* liberties. My Dad would sometimes spot quail as we were driving, stop the truck, pull out his shotgun and shoot them. Then it would be my job to run over, pull their heads off and take them home so we could clean and eat them.

Another recreational activity, fun but not terribly smart, was what we called "sledding," which didn't involve snow but instead meant a truck would pull you around a cleared field by a rope while you tried to balance on a piece of plywood.

CHAPTER 17

The area around Havelock had mostly been poor prior to the construction of Cherry Point in 1941. Turpentine and tar production for the Navy were important to the economy during the Nineteenth century, but as wooden ships had been gradually phased out in favor of steel vessels, a lot of the distilleries had turned to producing moonshine to make ends meet.

Cherry Point's primary World War II mission was training Marines for service in the Pacific, while the air station served as a base for anti-submarine operations. During the Korean War it provided aviators and air crewmen as well as maintenance and support personnel as replacements to forward aviation units; during Vietnam, Cherry Point deployed A-6 Intruder squadrons to the Far East and again provided a constant source of replacements for air crews.

During Operation Desert Storm, Cherry Point supported the deployment of numerous air squadrons. Since 9/11, Cherry Point Marines and Sailors have participated in strike missions and follow-on operations in Afghanistan. Cherry Point is regarded as one of the best all-weather jet bases in the world. Its runway system is so large that it serves as an alternate emergency landing site for the Space Shuttle.

Having a dad who is a Marine and living next to a military base has a definite effect on a kid. One of my earliest memories is living in Hawaii with my biological father and my mother, being three years old and watching "Popeye" on TV and eating spinach my mom cooked for me. One year my dad got a record player for me, and the only two records I had were "The Star Spangled Banner" backed by "The Battle Hymn of the Republic," and "The Marine Corps Anthem," backed by another military song.

According to my mother, when I was about two or three years old my dad was being reassigned by the Marine Corps so naturally he moved my mother, my sister Debbie and me with him to the new base. We headed out in our beat up station wagon and along the way had decided to stop at a motel. After checking in, we went to our room where my mother laid me on the side of the bed while she helped my dad bring some of our belongings in from the car. My sister Debbie, who was weary from the trip, had plopped down on the bed opposite the side I was lying on, which caused me to fly through the air. I landed on the floor with a thud and immediately began crying, as children do whether they're hurt or not. My mother came running in and scooped me up, rubbed the shoulder I had landed on, and kissed my boo-boo to make it feel better.

My mother said that for the next few days I walked around slouched over and leaning to one side. She thought I was kidding, as I was a natural born prankster, but eventually she suspected something might be wrong, so she took me to the base hospital where X-rays showed I had broken my collarbone.

On another occasion, while I was being baby-sat by my sister Deb, we were horsing around on the couch the way kids do. She would tickle me and make me almost pee my pants. Apparently, this one time while we were playing, someone had left crochet needles stuck down between the cushions with the points sticking up. As Debbie was tickling me, I flung my head backwards and heard a THWACK sound. When I sat up my sister was crying both from hysterics and laughter. The needles were stuck in my head and I looked like "My Favorite Martian!" Needless to say, we went back to the base hospital emergency room, where I was becoming quite the celebrity, as I had just been there for sitting in a pile of fire ants. Again, the X-rays showed that the needles had penetrated my scalp but not my skull, even though to this day some people question the doctor's finding.

Growing up in Havelock we observed military traditions. Every Nov. 10, the anniversary of the Marine Corps' founding, they would load all us kids onto school buses and take us over to Cherry Point, where there'd be a ceremony, we'd recite the Pledge of Allegiance, get a piece of cake, and get back on the buses and head back to school, where many of our teachers were former Marines. The school board had a few retired officers on it as well.

They'd also bring motivational speakers into school, just to address the boys, and they were invariably Marines. One speaker—he was a former POW in Vietnam, and all he wanted to talk about was killing the enemy, killing every gook you laid eyes on, and by the time he was finished we were like, "Where do I sign up?"

"You're only fifteen," they had to remind us. "Relax."

When the Vietnam War ended there was no noticeable effect in Havelock. The general population stayed gung-ho about military service. How could we not, when virtually everyone's father, uncle or brother was in the service?

CHAPTER 18

Havelock was basically a nice town to grow up in, even though we had no money, and racism was still prevalent, particularly among the older people. The pizza place I ate in still had segregated bathrooms.

Racism is part of life, but people's differences never mattered to me. I know, the south is supposedly the nexus of race issues in the United States, but you notice it everywhere you go. I learned to be accepting, I think, because being from a military family we moved around a few times and that exposed me to a lot of different people. One day you're in the majority, the next you're in the minority.

In Havelock, the black kids made up about forty percent of the school population, though none of them lived right in Havelock, only in the surrounding towns.

When we lived for about a year in Santa Anna, California, the high school I went to was eighty percent Latino, ten percent black and ten percent white, so I got to experience what it was like being the minority. Then for a while we lived in Millington, Tennessee, where my school was ninety percent black and five percent white.

I guess because I was mostly oblivious to racism, its presence always surprised me. One time, while working for DOE, I was sent to Augusta, Georgia. There were railroad tracks running through the center of town with a row of bars on either side of the tracks. I pointed out a bar on the left side of the tracks and was dissuaded from going there. "That's the black side of town," I was told.

But the place was jumping, there was music coming out, people seemed to be having fun. So I went to the left. I was the only white person in there, and all eyes were on me, but I didn't care. And, after the initial surprise, the other patrons didn't seem to care, either.

When I went to my thirty-year reunion at Havelock High School I noticed all the black guys were hanging out in front of the restaurant rather than inside. I asked them if they were coming in.

"Hell, no," I was told. "How many black people do you see in there?"

Enough said.

So sometimes people segregate themselves, particularly if that's how they're most comfortable. After I had enlisted in the Navy a bunch of recruits and I were taking a train from Raleigh to Navy boot camp in Orlando, and we were in the bar car, and after a few beers we started singing patriotic songs, and the other passengers started booing, cursing us and shouting insults.

We tried not to let it bother us, knowing unhappiness over the Vietnam War was still being felt, but it still stung a little.

There were sixteen of us on that train, ten white guys and six black guys, and even though everyone got along, when it was time to go to bed there were two areas for us, one with nine bunks and the other with seven. And the white guys all headed one way and the black guys headed the other. There was only one bunk left and that was at the back of the train, so I went and bunked with the black guys.

It didn't bother me, but I noticed how, given the choice, most guys would segregate themselves by race.

CHAPTER 19

When I graduated from high school in 1975, I had the opportunity for a college scholarship at Eastern Carolina University and had always loved science and scored well, but rather than attend college, I followed my stepfather's advice when he told me, "You should really serve your country."

I didn't know there was such a thing as a nuclear navy. The only thing I knew regarding the word "nuclear" was that there were bombs. I discovered the nuclear navy when I was placed in its service.

I was young and dumb, and I did whatever my dad or other authority figures told me to do. I just wanted to enlist, do my time and get back home to shore. I would've spent all my time peeling eggs if they had ordered me to.

My grandmother knew Adlai Stevenson, and she tried to get him to appoint me to Annapolis, but ultimately I decided to enlist in the Navy, because my dad said they had the best career training. The recruiter was more interested in impressing my dad than he was in me, and that's up whose ass he blew all his smoke. And when I got into the nuclear navy program he couldn't have been prouder, even though I had no idea what I was doing.

I had scored high on the Navy's proficiency test, which allowed me to attend Nuclear Power School, the best and most extensive training the Navy offered. I was designated as an electronics technician (ET) because of my score on the aptitude tests.

School for ETs, or "twidgets" as we were affectionately called by the other rates, took several months to complete, but Nuclear Power School was a year of training: one year in the classroom and half a year on a simulated sub, which was a reactor that had moved onto land.

The schoolwork was intense. At the time, the government said our training was the equivalent of half a million dollars in schooling. And what we were learning was classified, so you couldn't bring your homework back to the barracks with you. You did your homework in the classroom, weekends and evenings if you had to, and if you didn't log in for the required homework time they reported you as AWOL, and you risked losing a portion of the twenty-five cents an hour you were earning.

We studied nuclear physics, thermodynamics, physics, chemistry, electronics, electrical engineering, mechanical engineering and metallurgy. All crewmembers (or "bubbleheads" as the "surface pukes" called us) on a nuclear sub had to be cross-trained on all the ship's equipment.

Our motto was "two point five and survive." That was the GPA you needed to graduate. Sixty of us started school together. A year and a half later we had a graduating class of ten men.

I scored high enough that I was also trained to teach others, and that's how I spent my one year off the sub, teaching at Nuclear Power School.

CHAPTER 20

My family walked me to the bus stop to say goodbye, and my mother and sister started to cry, but my dad wanted to prepare me for what was ahead, so he was very direct. "Take a good look around here, because you ain't coming back here again," he told me.

He actually had a smile on his face, he was that glad to be rid of me. I shouldn't have been surprised; even on his deathbed he couldn't muster the fortitude to tell me he was proud of me, even though I knew he was.

When you tell people an anecdote like that they typically ask, "How did that make you feel?" How do I feel? When people ask me questions like these I really have to stop and think about the answer. I ask myself, *Who the hell am I? How do I feel about things?*

These questions are usually prefaced with casual talk in an attempt to get me to lower my "defense shields" and "let the real me come out."

Yeah, right.

People who know me well know that's not how I operate. Years of intense conditioning made me the way I am emotionally. My father and my stepfather were both Marines, and tenderness and "feelings" were not part of the program. Nor would it be allowed in mine.

My birth father I referred to as my father and my step-dad I referred to as my dad. Notice I didn't say I *called* them father or dad, oh Hell no. That was not in the program. I was raised to say "Sir, yes sir, no sir, right away, sir."

When I was about seven or eight my dad made a shocking revelation to me: Men don't kiss each other. You see, when I was growing up I used to kiss my father and my dad every night before going to bed. But that was when I was a kid. Now, I was informed, men shake hands. So every night before I went to bed I shook my dad's hand goodnight.

Another startling revelation was made clear to me at about that same time. All men were to wake up at "oh-dark-thirty." For you non-military types that means early in the morning, before the sunrise. My dad would open my door and flick my room light on. It was one of the overhead lights with no lampshade, just a bulb. He would yell, "Reveille! Reveille!", and I had to be up, dressed ready for school, room cleaned and bunk made. I learned that you didn't ask for any slack and you didn't expect any either.

My home life was quite normal in the beginning but somewhere soon thereafter it turned downward. (My mother will probably kill me when she reads this, but it is MY story and it was my life). It happened, that time is gone from me forever, and I can never get it back.

The gory details I won't go into, but I do recall some intense moments. The situation went bad when my sister Debbie eloped with her high school sweetie and moved out of the house. Needless to say my dad was very upset and read me and my younger sister, Terri, the riot act. Now with Debbie gone there was no one to protect me except my mother. And it got very dicey at times.

My dad liked to drink and sometimes he would drink the hard stuff which made him meaner than a junkyard dog. Many were the times when he would come home and fight with my mother. I would have to try to stop them from fighting while trying to calm my three younger sisters who were crying hysterically. One time I tried to stop them and my dad turned his rage on me. That was a big mistake on my part.

Then there was the time my mother had gotten the better of my dad and was choking him to the point where he was blue. It was all I could do, but I pried her fingers off of his throat. My mother got mad at me for not letting her finish the job.

Another horrific point was when a friend of my dad's, another Marine, sexually abused me. I was more afraid to tell my dad about the incident than I was mad about what had happened. I hated that bastard friend of my dad's and was openly disrespectful to him. My dad, hearing about my disrespectful attitude, called me out to the flight line at Cherry Point and threatened to kill me if I didn't straighten out.

My dad is dead now and unless they have VCRs with rewind and playback features for everything that's happened in someone's life, he'll never know what happened in mine.

It was very difficult not being allowed any PDEs (public displays of emotion). I would go off somewhere secluded to be by myself. I think that is why I became such a loner. I didn't trust people in general.

That would all change when I got to my sub, the Seahorse.

But first I had to get there.

Navy boot camp was in Orlando in summer, which couldn't have been any hotter. Electrician Technical School was in Chicago in winter, which couldn't have been much colder. Our barracks were so cold in Chicago, with the wind whipping off Lake Michigan, that we had an eight-inch-thick block of ice inside the window between our beds. So my bunkmate and I improvised and carved shelves into the ice and stored our beer and soda in there.

It was a weird time to be in the service because a lot of guys signed up for the GI Bill benefits, then tried to have themselves discharged so they could leave but still qualify for the bennies. They'd say they were gay, that they wet the bed or walked in their sleep— anything to get out with their benefits intact.

One of my earlier jobs was to assist with guys who were being discharged. "Where did they get these guys from?" we'd repeatedly ask each other, because there weren't only guys looking to get out with false problems. There were also legitimate drug addicts, sexual predators and lunatics.

The first thing you had to do when you got to the boat was to learn every system on the sub; cross training was essential, because you might have to make do if crewmen were lost. So in addition to learning how to run the reactor, I learned weapons control, fire control, ballast control, sonar, radar, damage control…every station and every system. Even when we were underway at sea we had mandatory training and maintenance work details. You pulled your weight because you were part of a team and because it was your job.

I was nervous about going down in a sub, being claustrophobic and all, but the Navy made the adjustment easier, because when I reported for active duty the sub was in dry dock. They literally settled it on chocks in an enormous holding tank and drained the water. Like anyone else my perspective of submarines had always been similar to how I viewed icebergs: I only envisioned them based on the small part that sticks out of the water.

Then they drain the tank, and the enormity of the vessel grabs you. A submarine is *huge*. Crews begin cutting holes in its sides to refuel it, because it's not like pumping diesel onto a battleship; you're talking about removing radioactive fuel rods and assorted machinery. The holes were at least thirty by thirty, so my first experiences on the Seahorse came courtesy of walking through its side.

When it was time to get underway for the first time I had a watchstation to man, so I was too busy to be nervous. Whenever I wasn't working or on watch I would lie in my bunk and read just to keep my mind busy, even though after all my schooling I had vowed never to read again. There was a vent over my bunk, over all the bunks, which blew air on you, helping to create the illusion that you were above the water.

Most of the time on board was either work or boredom, but when you hit the beach, it was party time.

CHAPTER 21

But before we hit the beach, some information on nuclear submarines is in order.

I served aboard The Seahorse, a sub in the Sturgeon-class, also known as the 637 class. Sturgeon-class subs were attack subs, and the work horses of the submarine attack fleet during most of the Cold War. After the dissolution of the Soviet Union, Sturgeons were phased out in favor of the Los Angeles and Virginia class subs, but we were the primary tools in tracking Soviet subs for about twenty-five years.

We fit twelve officers and ninety-five enlisted men on a vessel two hundred ninety-two feet long that sometimes stayed at sea for months at a time, and under water and ice for most of that time. Quarters, needless to say, were close.

I was anxious about being assigned to a sub because I was claustrophobic, but I got past it pretty quickly. I didn't have a choice, and after a while even the most unusual setting starts to feel routine.

Our job was tracking Soviet subs. Sometimes this meant locating them and following them through the ocean. Sometimes it meant keeping tabs on them a little closer to their home, though most of that information remains classified. (The hot part of the Cold War is over, but neither country has put their sub fleet to rest in the fifteen years since the Soviet Union fell apart).

It's important that readers understand that nothing divulged in my story is classified. Not that revealing what I did during my years of service to the country could possibly harm the United States in any way, but I wouldn't want to potentially put the people I worked with or guys that may be doing something similar today in jeopardy.

One time we followed a Soviet sub up the east coast of the United States, and because we were in its wake it didn't know we were there. We would always drag sonar behind us to detect Soviet subs, but they didn't, so we were able to tail them undetected.

Of course, they could always pull what we called a "Crazy Ivan," turn around and come straight at you. They did this in order to "clear their baffles" to ensure they weren't being followed. After following them for a while we finally put out an active sonar ping, and probably blew their sonar man's ears out, to let them know we were there. They heard that and immediately ran for open water.

Being an attack sub we were heavily armed. Sturgeon class subs typically carried four torpedo tubes for Mk-48 torpedoes; Harpoon missiles, an all-weather, over-the-horizon, anti-ship missile; Tomahawk missiles, long-range, all-weather, subsonic cruise missiles designed as a medium- to long-range, low-altitude missile; and Subroc missiles. The UUM-44 Subroc was the first and only submarine-launched long-range nuclear armed anti-submarine missile ever deployed by the U.S. Navy. Sturgeons carried as many as six UUM-44A missiles. We also had mines we could lay.

The Seahorse had the ability to surface through ice, with a rein-forced sail and diving planes capable of rotating all the way to vertical. To stay under water for months at a time we had a system that gener-ated oxygen by electrolysis of water in a system we called "The Bomb." It was a huge one cell battery configuration with one hundred volts of electricity applied across its two plates. Sometimes the voltage and the hydrogen produced would unintentionally meet and the result was an explosion, thus the nickname. Atmosphere control equipment included a CO_2 scrubber, which removed the gas from air and pumped it overboard, and a machine that used a catalyst to convert carbon monoxide into carbon dioxide, also removed by a scrubber, and bonded hydrogen produced from the ship's storage battery with oxygen in the atmosphere to produce water. Gases were removed and oxygen replenished by use of an oxygen bank located in a ballast tank. Fresh water was produced by an evaporator, while seawater was used to flush toilets.

Among the things the scrubbers were needed for was cigarette smoke. You'd think the last thing you'd want to do in a long-confined area is smoke, but like servicemen have traditionally done over the years we smoked like chimneys. And those powerful scrubbers cleaned the air so good that we used to kid that you couldn't even get a good bugger underway.

When it was time to test the boat to see how she was rigged for at-sea conditions, the Officer of the Deck would begin a pattern of dives ("angles and dangles," as we called the maneuver), the sub would slowly rise up and nose down underwater, bow first, then stern, to make sure everything was securely stowed while we were under way. While this was going on we'd break up cardboard boxes and use them to slide on the floor from one end of the compartment to the other. We would also tie a string taut from one side of the bulkhead to the other; as we descended and the hull compressed, the string would gradually slacken until it was lying on the floor.

For general submersion or surfacing, we used the forward and aft tanks, called Main Ballast Tanks (MBTs), which would open and fill with water to submerge. For quicker depth adjustments we used smaller Depth Control Tanks (DCTs), also called hard tanks due to their ability to withstand higher pressure.

There are actually two hulls on a nuclear sub. We lived and worked inside what is known as the pressure hull. The hull that you see on the outside of a sub completely covers the pressure hull. Having two hulls has a lot of advantages, not the least of which is that all the activity inside the pressure hull is muffled by the outer hull. (This is what the Soviets were listening for on their sonar, along with engine noise). Plus some equipment that isn't vulnerable to increased pressure can be mounted between the hulls, saving valuable space inside the pressure hull. If the sub is damaged, the outer hull can also take most of the damage, which doesn't compromise the sub's integrity, as long as the pressure hull is intact.

The pressure hull was made of thick steel with a complex structure and high strength reserve, and was separated into compartments; it has to be able to withstand a force of several million tons, so it's made perfectly round in cross-section to evenly distribute the pressure. If the shape isn't perfect the hull could bend, or even give way. So, all hull sections have to be welded without defects. It's one of the reasons subs are so expensive to manufacture; you don't want to send a crew down unless you're certain that the hull is as near to perfect as you can make it.

You'd watch the structure around you compressing as you descended and you'd think, *Thank God the sea's not getting in.* The deeper you would go, the more the hull would creak and slide around inside the outer hull.

But for every minute of excitement on a sub there are hours of boredom. Of course, it never escapes your mind that you're in a vulnerable position: under water or ice, powered by a nuclear reactor and carrying nuclear and tactical weapons, and keeping an eye on an enemy who's also keeping an eye on you.

During the Cold War, the United States and the Soviet Union both lost subs. The Soviets lost at least four submarines during this period: K-129 was lost in 1968 (which the CIA is rumored to have attempted to retrieve from the ocean floor with the Howard Hughes-designed ship Glomar Explorer; K-8 in 1970, K-129 in 1986 (which was the subject of the movie "Hostile Waters"), and Komsomolets in 1989. Other Soviet subs, including the K-19 (the first Soviet nuclear sub) were badly damaged by fire or radiation leaks.

We lost two nuclear subs during the Cold War: the USS Thresher was lost due to equipment failure, and the Scorpion was also lost, possibly due to a faulty torpedo. Some think what may have happened to the Scorpion, which sank of the coast of New England in the '60s, was a Crazy Ivan gone wrong; two subs cruising at the same depth can collide, but there's no way of knowing. God rest their souls while on eternal patrol. Amen.

One time we had a leak around the periscope, and I remember walking past the periscope column as the ocean poured in, thinking, "Lord, don't let those baby drain pumps fail," because if they fail, you're going to the bottom. But you try not to think about it, because there's nothing you can do except pray to "the man upstairs" who's calling all the shots.

Then there's the inexplicable. You know you're in open water, you know you're deep enough, you're cruising at full speed, and bam! You've hit something.

It happened to us once, so we surfaced to discover the fairwater planes, steel structures used to control depth, were bent. Solid steel—and they were bent like an aluminum can. We never did find out what we hit, but we had to return to port to have the planes repaired.

CHAPTER 22

After being cooped up for long periods at sea (and underwater for the most part), we really cut loose when we had shore leave.

One time when we were docked in Puerto Rico we decided to go to the beach, so we bought two gallons of rum and a case of Coke and took the bus to the nearest beach. Rum in Puerto Rico in those days was about ninety cents a gallon for the cheap stuff (or sailor-grade), so there was no shortage of it. We were lying on the sand, drinking rum and coke and enjoying ourselves, and somebody said, "Hey, let's go skinny-dipping!"

So in we went. We were swimming in the water, buck-naked, when somebody realized it was getting late and that we'd miss the bus back to base if we didn't hurry. So we raced out of the water, slipped our shoes on and ran for the bus, completely naked, still carrying our drinks. And that's how we got on the bus, which was also carrying civilians.

The bus driver was laughing, and we passed out drinks to the other riders, and nobody seemed to mind much that we rode the bus naked back to the base. The bus driver must've seen sub guys on liberty before. He said, "You guys must be from that sub that just got in."

On another leave in Puerto Rico we rented a bunch of mini-cars, little four-seaters that weren't very fast, and we drove all over the island deliberately bumping into each other with these little cars and laughing and racing up the side of a mountain. What a bad icon we would have made.

My friend Tony once received a $7,000 bonus and took $1,000 out for us, just so we could party all weekend on leave. We were both twenty-one years old and came from poor southern backgrounds. Neither of us had ever seen that much money before. We went drinking for a couple of days straight, and by the time we sloshed back to the boat I was actually relieved to be back on board. I remember thinking then, *Thank God we're going to sea, because I can't take another day of this.*

Of course, there were recreational activities at sea as well, besides smoking, though we all smoked incessantly. There was a Smoking Lamp on board, which harks back to the era of wooden ships. When the Smoking Lamp was lit we could smoke, which was most of the time unless we were handling weapons or loading diesel. I could get a case of cigarettes in those days, ten cartons for $30, and everyone did it, so it was hard to avoid taking it up. Half of my bedpan was devoted to storing cigarettes because you never knew when you were coming back when we went out and the last thing you wanted to have happen was to run out of smokes while underway. Even though these guys were your brothers, something as sacred as a cigarette could cost you a buck at sea, if you could find someone willing to sell theirs.

Sometimes the activities were more creative. I'm a member of the Blue Nose Club, which is what they call guys who have crossed the Arctic Circle. The Navy actually lists this as a credential on your record and issues you a laminated card to prove it. (They have a similar recognition for crossing the equator, called the Shellback Club).

On the ship recognition of this fact came in a different form.

All of the new guys, and there were a lot of us on the Seahorse, were known as "pollywogs." I was at my station when the collision alarm sounded. *How the hell did we hit something,* I wondered. *We're in open water.*

All the pollywogs were led to the mess area where the Chief-of-the-boat (COB) and the XO stood before us, dressed as King and Queen Boreas Rex. The Chief had a wig, a beard and a trident, just like King Neptune, while the XO had on a wig and a coconut shell bra. I have to admit, after being at sea for awhile, he actually looked pretty good to some of us.

They shackled and blindfolded us and smeared us with colored lard, then told us they were shaving our heads, which was actually done with an electric razor on a push broom. The falling broom hairs were a convincing effect.

Then we were seated in a tub filled with ice water, and the icy water was ladled over us. When it was my turn a charge was read against me: "Sailor, it's said that you've accused the Queen of wearing a jockstrap. How do you plead?"

"Not guilty," I answered.

"Liar, give him some Truth Serum", the king ordered.

So they squirted Truth Serum, some vile combination that tasted like fish oil, Tabasco and possibly motor oil into my mouth and ordered me to swallow it, which I did.

They repeated the charge about the Queen's jockstrap, this time I answered, "Guilty." Again the king called me a liar and ordered me to eat Polar Bear meat which was made up of sardines and peanut butter.

Again they asked how I pleaded, and I told them, "I'll plead anything you want as long as I don't have to eat that crap again."

So I was told I had to eat the cherry from the Royal Baby's belly, but I knew there weren't any babies on board. Instead it was one of the fat guys in the crew with a cherry in his navel, and his belly had been smeared with peanut butter and mayonnaise. I was placed in front of the baby with my hands cuffed behind me and still blindfolded. When I leaned in two guys pushed the back of my head with a plunger into the fat guy's belly and held me there until I pulled out the cherry with my teeth.

I was told to crawl over to the King and Queen, where my blindfold was removed and I spit out the cherry. Then my nose was painted blue (hence the Blue Nose Society) and I was forced to crawl through a pile of garbage.

The last part of the initiation was that I was allowed to shower, but the hot water valves had been turned off, so my only option was Arctic water. It was a quick shower, but it was still better than sleeping covered in food and garbage, because we only had a two-hour window every Monday to do our laundry, and I wasn't willing to smell that bad for that long.

Keeping the bunk clean was important, because the area was only 6 ft. x 2 ft. We'd slip some of our clothes between the mattress and the bedpan to keep them pressed and stuff everything else underneath inside the bedpan. On one trip the Captain decided that flushing our Trash Disposal Units (weighted sacks that we stowed all the wet trash in) was too dangerous because another sub had experienced difficulty getting theirs to sink, which made them easy for the Soviets to spot. So we were forced to stuff them under our bunks for the duration of our time at sea. Now that was truly a pain in the ass.

I had a lot of experience with TDUs because the COB hated nukes, so I was often one of the crewmen assigned to go into this narrow space where we stashed the wet garbage and dumped CO_2 candles and retrieved new ones. We'd have to slog through these bags of wet garbage to get to the fresh CO_2 candles, and I hated doing it every time.

Another ritual, less elaborate than the Blue Nose Club, was the official membership into the "bubblehead" fraternity. Membership into that coveted organization was sealed by the traditional "tacking" your "dolphins" on. "Dolphins" were the pin you wore on your uniform that distinguished you from everyone else in the service. Tacking was how they were attached to your uniform. All the qualified crew members lined up and punched you in the chest, right on your dolphins. The impact left a red indentation in your skin which you wore like a badge of honor.

Back in my time, surface sailors didn't have a surface warfare pin like they do now. Only bubbleheads got to wear them. (And let me warn you right here, only a *bubblehead* can call another sub sailor *bubblehead*. So if you get your butt kicked by a pissed off sailor, don't blame me).

A more common form of entertainment was drinking, even though alcohol is strictly forbidden in the Navy (The United States Navy is the only one in the world, I've been told, which bans alcohol on board). We were potentially at battle stations at all times, so we were expected to be perpetually sober.

And we mostly were sober. We never drank at sea except once when we went on a long mission and someone got the bright idea to make homemade wine using #10 tin cans of fruit. We'd put it in a polyurethane bottle, add yeast and de-ionized water, punch a hole in the top, run tubing from it, put it outboard the main condenser and let it cook six or seven weeks. Anytime someone had a birthday or it was a holiday, we'd get into the wine. Only guys who were on watch were truly forbidden, and of course the rest of us had to refrain from getting truly drunk. The senior guys made sure nobody had more than a small cup or two.

The Chiefs ("the goats," as we referred to them) would bring on bottles and bottles of Listerine. When I first saw this I thought to myself, *Man those guys must have some really bad breath problems.* Later on I found out that the bottles were really filled with Jim Beam and Johnnie Walker.

Two days out we'd run out of fresh vegetables and milk, and from there on it was nothing but "plastic cow" (powdered milk) and "bug juice," which was basically Kool-Aid. The coffee, meanwhile, had the consistency of maple syrup, but that stuff would keep you alert.

Most of the guys got tattoos at some point. It's a Navy tradition, and I intended to get inked as well. I was in Portsmouth, England, and I had six tattoos picked out. My first was going to be scorpions on my inner-arm. We went out drinking that night, and the evening was supposed to culminate with me getting inked. But I passed out and the guys forgot about it.

I never went as far as picking them out again. I think, deep down, I wasn't all that eager to mark up my body. At various times I also considered a butterfly for my chest, like the character Papillion, and my wife's name (though I would've had to cross that one out eventually). You'd see guys get all sorts of crazy pictures; I heard of one guy who had a propeller tattooed on each butt cheek.

I also saw some nasty infections from tattoos. One time when we were pulling into Portsmouth, England, we received notice that we were to pickup new crew members waiting for us there. One of the guys, a young kid, (Young? I was only twenty-one myself at the time).

had been waiting for a couple of days and in the meantime had gone to a tattoo parlor and gotten four tats, two on each arm. When he came aboard for the first time you could see his arms were bandaged with blood and pus oozing from his "wounds." And when I was hospitalized with my liver and other problems, the guy in the bed next to me had contracted Hepatitis C, and the doctors said it was from tattoos. His liver was cancerous, the cancer was spreading, and a liver transplant wasn't going to help him at this point.

CHAPTER 23

The stress of being at sea in a submarine got to some guys. The living space in the sub was very confined, and being you're under water there's not a lot to see. Everyone starts going stir crazy when they're confined for long periods of time under those conditions; some guys get it worse than others.

We had returned aboard the Seahorse to the base in New London, Connecticut, after more than a month at sea, and everyone permitted ashore was going ashore.

A mess cook, a big guy we called Lurch, came off the gangplank and immediately tried to untie our submarine from the dock. Then he walked over to another sub, The Tullibee, and tried to throw its gangplank in the water.

Something had snapped in his mind and Lurch had superhuman strength at this point. He then walked over to a phone booth and tried to topple it into the water, with someone inside it. Eventually, the wagon from the "funny farm' came and took him away. Supposedly, there was something in a letter he received that sent him over the edge, but no one knew for sure.

Something like that makes everyone feel vulnerable. In a confined area, things are contagious. For example, I was never seasick, but there were what we called "social pukers," guys who felt fine until someone else starting throwing up, and then they'd start. A friend of mine, Tommy King, used to get seasick so quickly that whenever he heard the order given to single up all lines, an order which meant that we were untying in preparation for going to sea, Tommy started getting sick and puking.

We had returned back to New London a few months later, a few of us went to the Enlisted Men's Club and lo and behold there's Lurch, dancing with girls and having a good time. Who knew we all could've gotten away just by acting nuts?

Even though the drinking was overlooked to a certain degree, drugs weren't tolerated at all. A friend of mine was stopped by MPs and they found a pot pipe and some marijuana in his jeep. For that infraction they took away his nuclear status and put him on a reserve carrier in Jacksonville, Florida.

It was beautiful in Jacksonville and the job was low stress; the ship almost never left the dock. I remember thinking; *I wish they would punish me like that.* Not that I used drugs or anything, but I could find other ways to get in trouble. Hell, according to the COB (Chief-Of-the-Boat) all I had to do was be alive and that was enough reason for him to give me crap all the time. Once, when we were in Roosevelt Roads, Puerto Rico, for weapons certifications, me and Vinnie, another nuke watchstander, were left in port for an entire weekend with only one responsibility; to watch the skipper's government car and ensure that is was there and ready for him when he got back with the sub and the rest of the crew. It seems that the skipper's wife was coming to Puerto Rico to join him for a week of R&R.

Sounded easy enough, and it was the first time I got a break and didn't have to go to sea with the boat since I arrived there. So as soon as the boat turned around the edge of the harbor and out of sight of the pier, Vinnie and I parked the car on the pier, rented a local oil-burner and headed to San Juan. We partied our butts off, stayed at some cheap hotels, went to the Bacardi factory (which is another story in itself) and just relaxed. Monday morning we made a mad dash back to the base to get there before the boat pulled back in. We got there just in time to see the Seahorse pulling around the bend heading back to the pier. Just then, Vinnie and I almost had a heart attack... *"Where was the frigging G-car?!"*

All of a sudden I heard this booming voice, "Centore, where is my frigging car?" It was the skipper, with a bullhorn, who had just realized that his car was not on the pier as he instructed. At that moment I couldn't decide whether I should run away, drown myself, or just act like nothing happened.

None of these options seemed appropriate so I did the only thing I could do, tell the truth. So I yelled back to the skipper, "I don't know."

Apparently the base Seabees, who were in charge of the G-cars, thought it was abandoned and had it towed. I was never left in port again after that incident.

Most of the guys on The Seahorse were professionals. I had heard that there was another sub in our squadron where all the nuclear technicians had been busted for drugs, and their nuclear division was being run by an E-4. We never had a problem like *that*.

CHAPTER 24

I re-enlisted after four years for a second four-year hitch. We were at Roosevelt Roads Naval Base in Puerto Rico at the time. Guys had the option of having their swearing-in ceremony anywhere they wanted; some guys wanted it in the torpedo tubes or the escape trunk, but I asked to be lowered over the side in a rubber raft with the Old Man, as we called the captain.

I was dressed in dungarees and Earth shoes as I climbed down the rope ladder and into the dingy. After he made me take the oath and swore me in, we stood and he extended his hand as though to shake mine, then threw himself overboard as though I'd pushed him. The whole crew was topside, watching and laughing. Then he extended his hand again so I could help him aboard, and he pulled me in, only I was still wearing my shoes and dungarees with my wallet in my pocket.

One guy, Leo Falardeau asked the skipper for a swim call and the old man said okay. Other guys started jumping into the water off the fairwater planes. There was a crew on another sub, the Dace, watching, and one of them later commented, "Man, you guys are the real Navy." I guess not every crew was as close as we were.

Sometimes we'd swim while at sea in the middle of the ocean when we'd find what the captain called "a flat spot." Guys would swim off one end of the sub while other guys would fish at the other end. I didn't go in the water. It occurred to me that the guys swimming might be a form of chum for the guys with the fishing poles.

It wasn't all fun, of course, and not just because we were playing cat and mouse with Soviet subs. The Captain was a great guy, but the COB was a bigot. There weren't a lot of black guys on subs, but as the senior enlisted man in charge of the crew, he seemed to single out the few we had for abuse.

We were pulling into Portsmouth, England, one time and there were three new crew members waiting on the dock, all black. After they boarded the COB read them the riot act, threatening to kick their asses if he heard any Black Power crap out of them. But they were just kids, they just wanted to serve and not make any trouble. It was that sort of unnecessary animosity that caused our crew, and probably a lot of other crews, to segregate when they socialized.

To my relief, the federal government truly seemed oblivious to color. We didn't socialize in general, but at work there were never issues about race. Of course, when I was at DOE we had DOE Secretaries like Hazel O'Leary, who is black, and Bill Richardson, who is Hispanic, and our Chicago Operations Manager, Marvin Gunn, is also black. But in the Navy those old stereotypes and animosities were always apparent.

CHAPTER 25

While assigned to work as an instructor on the prototype in upstate New York, I was "offered" the position of Division Leading Petty Officer (LPO).

My chief petty officer said the two senior guys he'd offered the job before me had declined. The first was a short-timer—nearly at the end of his hitch and reluctant to take on responsibility. The second followed his lead, saying, in effect, "If he doesn't have to do it, I don't have to do it." This prompted the Chief to tell me, "If you tell me you're not going to do it, I'm going to personally kick your ass right here."

So, maybe "offered" isn't the best description of the exchange. I took the job, but there was a lot of stress involved. I was working as an instructor at the age of twenty-three, and married with three kids.

I was about to be betrayed by my government for the first time.

Before, I'd been essentially responsible for myself. Being LPO meant scheduling all the preventive maintenance, which meant knowing who was available for each task, some of which were daily, some monthly and others quarterly, and knowing what phase the reactor was in at all times. Being LPO also meant scheduling the watch. At sea it meant having eight men under you; working on the prototype it meant scheduling for fifteen men.

I was enjoying working as an instructor and took special pride in helping guys through the academy who were unlikely candidates, the tough cases. I was inspired by the instructors I'd had several years earlier; they clearly were dedicated to producing quality nukes, even if it meant a lot of effort on their part. An instructor might be tempted to increase his graduation rate by pushing through unqualified candidates, but all I saw were instructors who pushed themselves hard to make us better, regardless of how much extra time it took them. I remain friends with one of my instructors to this day, and we've worked together in several states at different nuclear plants over the years.

(Plus an increased graduation rate wouldn't mean much if you were producing "house loads," as we called them. Each switch on the ship's electrical panel controlled certain functions, essential and non-essential. Non-essential circuits were known as "house loads," and nukes deemed as such weren't useful in any practical sense).

One such individual was this nice kid who didn't talk much and seemed kind of slow. But I worked with him over and over until he got it, and on his last day he finally passed his oral boards. Suddenly he was all smiles and I couldn't shut him up. But I had helped him get through.

Learning how to operate a nuclear reactor on a submarine was only part of the process learned working at the prototype. Learning how to work as a team and to understand all the linguistic shorthand was also essential. Working at the prototype, the language is very formal and the chain of command very strict. When you're out at sea, those chains get shortened and the language becomes shorthand and acronyms, and you learn to react much more quickly.

For example, one time at the beginning on a long deployment on the Seahorse, someone at squadron command who was running us through drills decided to order a reactor SCRAM, which was an emergency shutdown. So we ran the SCRAM drill and immediately started sinking. The Seahorse was too heavy, and without our reactor we had no power. We were dropping at a rate of one hundred feet per minute.

The Old Man came into the control room and yelled, "Secure from the drill, Reactor operator, Fast SCRAM recovery," which means restarting the reactor roughly five times faster than normal. I had it operating in less than a minute and we recovered, but we were less than five minutes from Test Depth, the depth at which the boat had been previously certified to go, and ten minutes from Crush Depth, the depth at which there were no guarantees you would not be crumpled like an aluminum can in a compactor.

On the prototype that exercise would have taken so long, Crush Depth would've been inevitable. Then again, Fast SCRAMs weren't practiced on the prototype, so it's useless to speculate. But at sea, seconds wasted could be the difference between life and death, so the sooner you learned the shorthand and how to anticipate, work as a team and react, the safer everyone was.

Incidentally, SCRAM is an acronym, but it's an unlikely one. Supposedly it dates to the days when the control rods had to be manually pulled from the reactor by ropes, thus starting it up. When shutting down the reactor in an emergency, rather than trying to lower the control rods slowly, the ropes were simply cut with an ax. SCRAM stands for Stanley the Control Rod Ax Man, because it was some guy named Stanley's job.

Take it for what it's worth. As we often said in the Navy, the difference between a fairy tale and a Navy story is this: fairy tales begin with, "Once upon a time…" and Navy stories begin with, "Hey, this is a no-shitter…"

CHAPTER 26

I came home one day from my shift as an instructor at the prototype to find a note from my wife on the table telling me goodbye. There I was, with three kids, ages four, two and one, and she'd waited until my most recent paycheck was deposited, cleaned out my checking account, frozen my savings account and left me to raise three kids by myself.

We had married when I was eighteen and training in Chicago. She was only sixteen when we married. She was my high school sweetheart, the first girl I'd been intimate with, and I sent most of my $80 bi-weekly paycheck home to her when I first joined the Navy. After we married I moved out of the barracks and into an apartment, and my oldest child, Christina, was born the following year.

Everything happened so fast, it seems like a blur now, but at the time it was like every hour took an eternity to pass. But, before I knew it, I was twenty years old, married, an E-4 in the service assigned as a reactor operator aboard an attack submarine, and a father of two. We didn't have much money, being an E-4 in the service in the mid '70s. I think I made about $600 a month. That was to pay for rent, utilities, food, car, gas, everything. There was never much left over, if any at all. But we were a happy little family, my wife would sew all the kids' clothes and I would fix our only vehicle, a 1975 GMC pick-up. I loved that truck.

Eventually the time came when The Seahorse was beginning to go on long deployments. Things were heating up with the Russians and there was turmoil in the Middle East. My wife and I decided she and the kids should move home with her parents in Virginia and I would move back into the barracks. Unbeknownst to us this would prove to be a bad mistake. I was gone all the time, The Seahorse was averaging three hundred twenty days a year at sea. We would pull into port on a Friday afternoon, shut down the reactor and set down liberty by dinner time. Since my family was not in the immediate area I always volunteered to take the first duty rotation which allowed my married shipmates with family in the area to visit.

Then, without fail, orders would come down from squadron. The Seahorse was to begin preparation for getting underway, a Russian sub would be spotted somewhere in the pond tracking a "boomer," also known as a ballistic missile sub. All liberty would be cancelled, we would have to begin the long, grueling task on pre-startup checks on the reactor control equipment—the same damn reactor that I had just shut down, after running it constantly for six weeks.

Then we would go to sea for what seemed like forever, until we would find our quarry. Now the games would begin. We would track the Russian boat for as long as we could while making sure that nobody was tracking us in the process. Once we tracked a Russian attack sub off the coast of Florida for about 30 days, then were finally ordered to get rid of her. The way to get rid of them is to let them know you are there, had been for some time, and had a firing solution plotted in with a warshot Mk48 torpedo loaded and ready to fire. They way you old them this was by putting a high-powered "ping" from active sonar in the water and blasting their sonarmen off the "stacks." The Soviets would forget about trying to be quiet, go to flank speed and head for sea and deeper water. We would follow for awhile to make sure she was gone.

I was finally assigned to shore duty as a training instructor in Ballston Spa, N.Y. The Navy had a nuclear prototype school which was a land based nuclear engine room of a sub. Here they trained new recruits before letting them go out to the fleet. It usually took a nuke anywhere from one and a half to two years to complete all the training before he was allowed to go out to the fleet. I finally didn't have to go to sea and I got to be with my family everyday, which had grown by one more as we recently had a third child.

My pay still stunk, but with the bonus the Navy paid me we were able to put a down payment on a home. It was an old farm home and when I say old, I mean OLD! It had newspaper stuffed in the walls for insulation, the sink drained right out the wall to the outside. I had to heat-wrap it to allow us to use the sink in the winter. We had a potbelly stove in the kitchen and an old coal burner in the basement. It wasn't much of a basement, more like a cave. There was a four stall house barn, a riding area and a four acre pasture. And it was only one mile from my job.

In the winter my wife took a job with a popular tax preparation company. This seemed to work out well as we needed the extra money, and I would take care of the kids after getting home from my military job. My wife worked for a guy who would eventually become my friend. Whenever I went to see her at work or pick her up I would see him and we would talk about this and that. I had no idea what he had planned for me and my family.

Apparently, this "friend" whom I shall call Jody, (my military brothers will know what I mean by that) had decided that he was going to have his cake and eat it, too. While he was engaged to a girl from his hometown in Buffalo, he was working on having sex with my wife. Eventually this snake got his way as I was to find out from friends of mine. One evening I was supposed to meet her at Bingo with a neighbor of ours. My wife showed up late and I asked her were she was, already knowing the answer. Of course, she lied to me which infuriated me. I got up, left the Bingo hall and headed for my truck to go home.

My wife came running after me trying to stop me. I told her to leave me alone, then I begged her to go away. Then we got physical. Not a moment I'm very proud of, but it happened. Shortly thereafter, we decided that I would take the kids to visit her parents which would give us a chance to work things out between us.

I drove the children to my in-laws, said good-bye and drove back to New York. When I got home I remember it was a bright, warm, sunny day. I went inside and there was nobody home. Strange, I thought. Then I saw a piece of paper on my kitchen table and picked it up. As I started reading it I felt as though somebody was punching me in the stomach and the head at the same time.

The note said she was leaving me, that she was not good enough for me and I would be better off without her and there was no way to contact her. I went nuts looking for her and could not find her anywhere. I decided to get my kids back, so my first stop was family court to get temporary custody, which back in 1981 was unheard of for a man. Then I drove to Virginia to get my kids.

When I got back to New York I started to do some assessment of my situation and realized that my wife had taken off and left me penniless. Now I have no wife, no money, and three little kids to take care of; all while trying to keep up with my job with the Navy.

I had leave coming to me, and I took it, but I couldn't afford to hire a sitter for my children. For a while I had a woman down the road watching the kids, and she did it for very little, but the arrangement was temporary. Eventually, I took the kids to stay with my mother, but by then the Navy had given me an ultimatum: either go back to the fleet as a regular ET, as my nuclear designation would be taken away; or take an honorable discharge.

It broke my heart to be forced to make a choice between two bad options, and it broke my mother and stepfather's hearts. All this time the Navy had talked about itself as a family, and after six years of service they wanted to throw me out because I needed to care for my children?

I took the honorable discharge.

One day the Chief is hammering at you, and the next he's your buddy asking if you want to re-enlist. There was always this duality, that they were on you but they were also looking out for you. Discovering that when things were difficult they'd toss me aside was disheartening.

Eventually, my wife and I would sit down and discuss divorce arrangements. She told me that the guy she ran off with wanted her very much, but he didn't want any of her kids. I said I would arrange for her to go to family court and sign over full custody to me; then she could go and do whatever she wanted. And so we did. We went to family court in Saratoga N.Y. where my wife signed the papers giving me full custody of our three children.

After getting out of the service, I moved to Long Island, NY and went to work for Long Island Lighting Co. Several years passed, then one day my daughter cuddled up next to me, weeping softly. I asked her what was wrong and she said she wanted her mommy. I literally felt my heart rip a bit at that moment. I didn't know what to say, so I said the only thing a daddy knows how to say to his little girl. *I'll try.*

Eventually, and after years of not having any communication with my estranged wife, we finally made contact. The more my daughter saw her mom the more she wanted to be with her. Finally, not able to take the hurt anymore, I asked her mother if my daughter could come live with her. And that was that. My ex made sure that anytime I wanted to see my daughter she would have a prior engagement to go to that would preclude her from visiting me.

Then one day, one of the most staggering blows I have ever had to deal with came in the form of a phone call from my ex. She wanted her new hubby, the guy who she ran off with, my Jody, the guy who did not want any kids and in particular mine, to adopt my daughter so she could change her last name. She tried to give me some bullshit excuse of it being for educational financial opportunities. Horse-hockey!

I called a lawyer in Buffalo who informed me that he would be happy to take my five grand, but in the end I would lose anyway. Having to admit defeat, I asked to speak to my daughter again. I told her I didn't like this but she would always be my little girl. I didn't realize it would be many years before I got to see my daughter again.

So that's how and why my Navy service came to an end. It was a traumatic time in my life, but I left the service with great memories. We were a tight-knit unit on the Seahorse. We always prided ourselves on honor and Navy tradition, of doing what you're asked with no complaints or bravado. To find that the Navy has no use for us if there are problems was more than disillusioning, it was devastating.

The best thing that came out of my Navy service was the guys who I met in the Navy. We stayed close. We're still in contact after all these years. It's a brotherhood, and I can't put my finger on why, but there was something special about the experience of serving together. From the moment I had boarded that ship I knew I was finally home. I had found my universal family. Even as this book goes to print, I attended a reunion with my old shipmates in Charleston, SC, which was our home-port.

And there was my nuke training, which gave me some very specialized career options after leaving.

CHAPTER 27

After I left the Navy I needed a job, so I went to work for LILCO at the Shoreham Nuclear Power Plant on Long Island in 1981 for $10 an hour, but the plant was badly mismanaged. It seemed they were only interested in selling it, not operating it, so I quit and took in a job in California working at a nuclear power plant for Southern California Edison.

I liked living in California with the year-round beautiful weather. But something was always missing. There weren't any real old-fashioned family gatherings like back East, probably because most of us had come from the East and left families behind. The adults seemed to spend all their recreation time apart from their children. Not that I was ever the biggest family man, but the whole atmosphere seemed strange to me. So I began looking for another job.

Eventually, I started my own business as a nuclear consultant, flying all over the country to provide training and service at nuclear plants to the highest bidder. We were known throughout the industry as "Road Whores," because our only guiding principle was making money for our services.

I built a home in the Hamptons on Long Island, but I was never home. I had traveled across the United States from east to west and south to north, working all the while. Finally in 1992, a friend invited me to work for the DOE as Regional Response Coordinator at Brookhaven Lab. It was a fifty percent pay cut, but I took the job just so I could have some stability in my life.

Even though my Navy experience had ended unflatteringly, I wasn't concerned about working for the federal government. I had no reservations. This is the Executive branch, I told myself. They take care of their employees.

CHAPTER 28

I was a one-man team at Brookhaven Lab when I joined DOE to work there in 1992, with the responsibility of implementing a program that, while it existed in theory, had never truly been established.

My primary responsibility was re-introducing RAP to federal, state and local agencies that might require our expertise. It was a Pandora's Box, of course; any time you tell people that they can contact you night and day under any circumstances, they will. As a result I was always on call, though the inconveniences of being RAP's Regional Coordinator were nothing compared to the later relentless insanity of coordinating a NEST team. We went out on RAP calls several times each month, with nothing scarier than possible radiological contamination involved in any of them.

DOE had divided the country into eight regions, but this being the federal government, FEMA had divided the country into ten, so in coordinating with authorities I had to meet with the representatives from the three FEMA regions, known as RACs (Regional Assistance

Committees). We would gather with representatives from the federal, state and municipal governments as well as people from the private utilities that produced electricity from nuclear reactors.

There are thirty-three nuclear reactors in the region, so quite a few utilities rely on nuclear power, plus each reactor conducts a major exercise every few years to rehearse response to an accidental radiation release. For these exercises I would bring scientists with me from Brookhaven for on-site training, though the coordination of such exercises was my responsibility alone. Needless to say, this being the federal government there was a lot of paperwork when I wasn't actually in meetings or on exercises.

I remember when the Chernobyl meltdown occurred, DOE tracked the resultant radioactive plume as it floated around the world and dispersed using one of its emergency response assets known as ARAC (Atmospheric Release Advisory Capability). ARAC was a large super-computer built and maintained at Lawrence Livermore national Lab near San Francisco. They had the capability to monitor events that far away.

Opened in 1947 on Long Island in Upton, New York, Brookhaven National Lab is a multi-program national laboratory operated by Brookhaven Science Associates for the DOE.

Brookhaven's staff is approximately three thousand scientists, engineers, technicians and support staff and over four thousand guest researchers annually. Only about thirty-five of us worked directly for DOE; the rest are contractors. Six Nobel Prizes have been awarded for scientific discoveries made at Brookhaven Lab.

Brookhaven's jobs for DOE include conceiving, designing, building and operating facilities for DOE; carrying out research in long-term, high-risk programs; developing advanced technologies that address national needs; and disseminating technical knowledge, educating scientists and engineers, and encouraging scientific awareness in the general public.

Discoveries at Brookhaven Lab include L-dopa, which is used to treat Parkinson's disease; magnetically-levitated trains; using X-rays and neutrons to study biological specimens; Thallium -201, which is used in heart stress-tests; Technetium 99m, used to diagnose heart disease; and X-ray angiography.

Most people think of DOE as being exclusively about regulating the energy industry in the United States, but that's only one of its functions. All nuclear weapons deployed by the Department of Defense (DOD) are actually on loan from DOE, which has federal responsibility for the design, testing and production of all nuclear weapons. DOE in turn uses contractors to carry out its responsibilities; including the design of the nuclear components of the weapon, which is who the majority of the employees at Brookhaven are.

DOE was created by President Jimmy Carter in 1977, putting disparate organizations under the umbrella of one department. DOE has four national security priorities: insuring the integrity and safety of nuclear weapons; promoting international nuclear safety; advancing nuclear non-proliferation; and, continuing to provide safe nuclear power.

My responsibilities fell under the categories of nuclear safety and non-proliferation. Whereas RAP teams had been primarily about contamination issues, NEST was purely counter-terrorism.

I hadn't minded the fifty percent pay cut when I joined DOE, because I still had tremendous loyalty to my government. Plus it put an end to the "Road Whore" years, of flying all over the country to fix nuclear plants, living in a compound and only coming home so I could pack up again and hit the road. And Brookhaven was nearly in my back yard.

But, as with any bureaucracy, there was interference from superiors who didn't necessarily understand the work we were doing, or care that they were interfering with it. I did what I was told whenever possible, but sometimes I declined to cooperate.

For example, when the tall ships were sailing into New York Harbor in 2000, there was heightened security. Who knew what was coming into the harbor in one of those ships? An Air Force Colonel in Washington ordered me to get him and his staff access to NYPD's Tactical Operations Center for the day. Maybe he wanted to look like a hero if we found a nuke, but I wasn't having any part of it, and neither was the FBI. "If we need them, we'll reach out to them," my FBI contact responded. "We just want to work with you and your people."

The colonel was so pissed off at me when I told him he wasn't welcome, but I told him, I'm thinking, *You're pissed at me when its not my call?The local FBI made the final decisions on such things and he knew it!*

Special Forces guys are great if you want to blow up a building or shoot a hundred guys, but if you want to detect and identify a nuclear device, they're out of their environment. And I was more than a little suspicious of their presence on NEST operations. *Maybe they're not here to protect us. Maybe they're here to shoot us in case we're captured and the terrorists want information out of us.* In any event, it was always a hairy situation when you went into a potential gunfight without a weapon or ballistic protection.

Fortunately, we were never fired on during a NEST operation.

The secrecy in our contact with Washington was amazing: most of our conversations were encrypted, and I had to take calls in a small room in a remote building we called "The Vault" on a special phone. We had other euphemisms for it—The Cone of Silence, The Bat Phone—but in front of the other agency representatives we were very serious, all business.

I was envious of the guys in Washington, who only had to pick up their phones, push a special button and their calls were automatically encrypted. I had to go to a separate building that was monitored and swept for bugs, and lock myself away in a soundproof room just to take a call from Washington.

I had to maintain this air of propriety and a certain stature, because of the secrecy and because I was in charge of so many civilians at Brookhaven Lab, but it killed me, because it wasn't my personality. I wanted to be able to joke with people, but working for the government you learn that you need a certain air of dignity at all times.

In the early years of my tenure with DOE, I had decided to run a readiness drill for the Region One RAP team. Prior to running the drill, I was informed that DOE had a Memorandum of Understanding with the U.S. Coast Guard in that, should the need arise where we had to be transported somewhere in the region quickly, that Coast Guard would oblige by providing helicopter transport between Brookhaven Lab and the incident site. They had provided us with a twenty-four-hour hotline that we were told to call in case of such an event. So I decided, *What the heck, let's give it a try.*

Much to my surprise, the individual answering the phone on the USCG end had no idea of what we were talking about and had no intention of sending a helicopter to anywhere to pick up a *what?! RAP Team! Is this some kind of joke?!* I could understand his frustration and distrust in the call; I always hated using that term when people asked who we were, and it always opened the flood gates for wisecracks and snide remarks.

During the years preceding the terrorist attacks, Congress recognized the need to develop better coordination between the many different agencies that could be called upon to support such a situation. Congressmen Nunn, Lugar, and Domenici drafted and pushed into approval the act known as the Nunn-Lugar-Domenici bill (NLD program) that mandated requirements for federal agencies interaction and pre-planning with state and municipal agencies that have a responsibility for responding to a terrorist attack on American soil. The bill also provided training for local responders. The federal teams were allowed to train local responders on specialized equipment, but were not allowed to provide funding for the local responders to buy the new equipment. It was like, *Here is this great equipment, this is what it can do for you, however, you can't have it!*

Also part of the NLD program was the establishment of Joint Terrorists Task Force (JTTF). Although the name sounds daunting, what it implies is the coalition of agencies that would respond in the event of a terrorist attack in a municipal area. It provided for pre-planning and coordination of efforts before an incident occurred in an American city. I was a member of the New York City, Philadelphia, Boston, and Washington, DC JTTFs representing DOE. At the time, DOE had a major response role in the event of a terrorist attack involving a nuclear device (nuclear bomb) or radiological material (dirty bomb), as DOE owned, funded, equipped, staffed, and trained the members of the NEST team.

CHAPTER 29

RAP had been a great responsibility, but the transition to a NEST team after 9/11 truly tested my endurance. I was on call every day during that time, twenty-four hours a day. The stress was non-stop, and with typical Washington inefficiency there were far too many chiefs and not enough braves. NEST deployment suffered, not only because we took directions, sometimes seeming arbitrarily, from unnamed or uninformed government officials, but my team had a literal dual chain-of-command. I was operationally responsible to Washington while my personnel matters where handled by local management at Brookhaven.

My supervisors at DOE headquarters in Washington were military men taking their two-year administrative turn in Washington, where they played war from behind a desk rather than on a battlefield. I would get to know one, and he'd move on without any advance notice. Then I'd have another career military officer telling me what to do, regardless of his understanding of the team's responsibilities.

At Brookhaven my chief responsibility was coordinating my team, which in true bureaucratic fashion included a lot of paperwork. They wanted the eight NEST team leaders in Washington every few weeks for debriefing and mandatory paperwork, but I could hardly get my work done from Long Island, never mind taking a train to DC. I was running non-stop with my NEST responsibilities; maybe they viewed visiting Washington as an important assessment tool, maybe they just wanted us under their thumb. But I was usually too busy to accommodate that request.

They did acknowledge my dedication and hard work, in their backhanded fashion, with a monetary award of $2,000. It was a fraction of what the brass awarded themselves for what they perceived to be a job well done, and I had no time to spend the money they gave me, but I didn't do my job for the money anyway. Good thing.

The letter of commendation read, in part:

"Mr. Steve Centore has maintained the highest operational tempo in the Department of Energy/National Nuclear Security Administration Emergency Response community. Starting with an immediate response to the vicious attack on the World Trade Center, he led a team to assist local responders in assessing radiological hazards in the rubble. Without respite, his team quickly configured for continuous operations in support of the Federal Bureau of Investigation to locate and intercept any possible subsequent attack. He continues to enthusiastically support an interagency effort to assist New York City in developing new plans for thwarting and responding to future acts of terrorism. He dutifully rises to meet national security challenges every day, demonstrating real personal skill, unquestionable reliability and effectiveness. Mr. Centore's leadership, innovative management skills, and interaction with federal, state, and local law enforcement and emergency management personnel has been a model that will be replicated throughout the Department. This direct response to a terrorist attack is being incorporated throughout the Department's emergency response community. His outstanding performance in the terrorist response and potential attack is outside the scope of his official duties and warrants special recognition."

I was heading to Washington when my first serious physical symptom occurred in May, 2005, when I twisted my back boarding the Amtrak train in Penn Station. In retrospect it's a surprise that something within me didn't give out sooner, either mentally or physically. But I was trained to push on. They wouldn't ask it of me if they didn't think I could do it. They certainly wouldn't ask anything of me that wasn't absolutely necessary.

My faith in the institutions I worked for and the nation I served had been tested before. Yet, that faith was about to be torn apart.

CHAPTER 30

The panic attacks took me by surprise, but so did DOE's response to them.

I didn't tell my supervisors specifically what was wrong with me, but I told my boss at Brookhaven Lab that I wasn't feeling well. Verbal communication, I later realized, isn't sufficient because an unscrupulous person can later claim to have no memory of that conversation, which is precisely what he said to me in August when I reiterated the complaint.

"This is the first I'm hearing of it," was his response.

I was stunned. *I've been telling you I'm not feeling well for months, and now you're going to pretend this is the first you're hearing about it?*

But I still trusted my supervisors then.

DOE, on the other hand, was very careful to put every communication with me in writing. (Except for certain ones, I was to learn later on). Being naïve and loyal I assumed this was merely Standard Operating Procedure, but there's actually a far more practical and cynical reason for putting everything in writing: they can build a case against you when they decide to terminate you AND blame you for the termination.

Meanwhile the workload continued unabated. There were NEST regions and corresponding teams that had a fraction of the responsibility we had. Some regions had states with a cumulative population that was less than that of my home county, Suffolk.

Two or three times a year we were also asked to attend conferences in Las Vegas to compare notes and review procedures. I never cared for these conferences because I had too much to do, and too little was accomplished when we got together. It wasn't just that the meetings ended with no resolution to our conflicts over procedures, it was that we had the same conflicts and the same lack of resolution every time we got together.

I didn't want to be in Las Vegas. I was in no mood to have fun. I had too much on my plate, and each conference wasted more valuable time.

They were disappointed when I couldn't attend one conference because I had to testify before the grand jury in the John Ford case, which I mentioned earlier. I have a responsibility to my actual job, I reminded them, but I knew it was another mark against my record.

But my record was otherwise stellar. Even though I was the whipping boy whenever something in my region went awry, as in the Palermo Senator case, I was still one of DOE's golden boys because my team pulled such a disproportionate share of the load, and did its job well. My RAP program had been commended by officials at every level of government, from the state, county and municipal officials we trained up to the brass at DOE. My performance appraisals during my fourteen years directing both the RAP and NEST operations were consistently superior.

Some examples of "love letters" I received for my work at DOE: "*Presented to Steven M. Centore: In recognition of your assistance to New York City following the attack on the World Trade Center, September 11.2001. Your role in the successful response of the Radiological Assistance Program Team and the Fire Department from the U. S. Department of Energy's Brookhaven National Laboratory demonstrated your dedication to your profession, the Department of Energy, the City of New York, the State of New York, and the United States of America.*" Spencer Abraham, Secretary of Energy

"Presented to Steven M. Centore: In recognition of the efforts made toward revitalizing Brookhaven Area Office (BRO) participation in the Radiological Assistance Program (RAP) as the Region One Coordinating Office. Your display of professionalism in reestablishing effective working relationships with federal, state, and local emergency response organizations has been critical to BHO meeting its RAP responsibilities." Cherri J. Langenfeld, Manager, DOE

"Mr. Centore provided information to one hundred thirty local, county, state and federal radiological response personnel. The responders really appreciate his keen insight into nuclear terrorism and how they might be affected by a WMD incident. The Commonwealth's Radiological Protection Program has definitely been enhanced, which will undoubtedly raise the safety margins for the general public. The workshop participants and organizers are forever grateful," from the Pennsylvania Emergency Management Agency's Director of Bureau Operations.

"I would like to take this opportunity to thank you for the outstanding support and performance you displayed during the Ingestion Pathway October 1996 federally graded exercise. Your dedication and professionalism contributed to the success of the drill and resulted in obtaining an excellent rating by the exercise evaluator," from the Director of the Delaware Emergency Management Agency.

"I would like to thank DOE for the assistance provided by Mr. Centore. He traveled to Pennsylvania on short notice and remained on site until it was assured the situation was under control. This was especially valuable this time because the Regional Health Physicist was recovering from surgery and was unable to respond to the incident. This was an excellent example of a coordinated Federal response to a radiological release, and of interagency cooperation and mutual assistance," from the EPA's Regional Radiation Representative.

"A Certificate of Special Congressional Recognition (is) presented to Steve Centore in support of World Trade Center Operations, in recognition of outstanding and invaluable service to the community," from Congressman Felix Gruici.

I was a top level performer, recognized, rewarded and respected. But just as I had experienced in the government before when personal issues interfered with their skewed definitions of responsibility and loyalty, rather than address the problems I was having they opted to punish me for bringing my problem forward.

It shouldn't have come as a surprise to me because the administrators at Brookhaven Lab were notorious for sabotaging employees they had problems with, even when the problems weren't the fault of the employee. I worked with one guy who kept nodding off because the medication he was taking for acid reflux disease made him drowsy. They kept putting him on report, built a case against him, and dismissed him for dereliction of duty.

He sued and won, getting his job back and receiving his back pay, and we silently cheered his victory. And as to rub salt in an open wound, the individual went on to become a senior manager in the DOE's counter-terrorism program in DC.

My supervisor did little all day except got to meetings and walk the halls to monitor people's conversations. Talk about a lack of trust and a waste of his abilities (whatever they allegedly were). He would report any information he thought would be useful to upper management. We would bait him by making up false stories to see if they tried to punish people for things that never actually happened, which sounds like fun, but people's careers hung in the balance based on his perceived observations.

Out of necessity that summer I took a week to visit my mother in Illinois. I didn't even think about work that week, and it was the last week I would have for many months without a panic attack. But I didn't make the connection; after all, everyone's more relaxed on vacation.

As soon as I returned to work the panic attacks resumed, sometimes one right after another. Sometimes there was a trigger, like seeing a death in a movie or something traumatic on TV, but often the only trigger was my mind, unconsciously recalling some horrific scene from Ground Zero.

After Dr. Buono prescribed my meds to combat the panic attacks, ordered thirty days' bed rest and diagnosed my PSTD, on Sept. 12, 2005 I reported his diagnosis to my supervisor at Brookhaven, and they referred me to a psychiatrist in their Employee Assistance Program.

Again, I trusted DOE's judgment. That was a mistake.

CHAPTER 31

I asked my wife to take Dr. Buono's note to work. That was on Tuesday. On Wednesday, the next day, a registered letter arrived from DOE informing me that I was being reported as Absent Without Leave (AWOL) which meant loss of pay. This meant that now, on top of everything else, I had to worry about how to pay my bills and feed my family.

My supervisor recommended I call the Employee Assistance Program (EAP) which I did. They referred me to a psychiatrist in DOE's EAP program, so I made an appointment to go and see him.

I wasn't enthusiastic about telling anyone my problems, and I wasn't much on talking about my innermost thoughts in general. But I was willing to follow procedures if they would help me get back to work sooner. These feelings of anxiety and despair, the paralyzing feelings of dislocation and confusion—I had to find a way to make them stop.

My first visit with DOE's psychiatrist wasn't particularly useful.

He fell asleep during my first session, so I took a nap, too. I was having a lot of trouble sleeping, so it seemed like a good opportunity.

When he fell asleep during our second session I woke him up, and he admitted that he couldn't help me, that my case was too difficult, but that he would be willing to work with me as a private patient.

This was the guy DOE wanted me to see? He was just trying to get more money out of the deal, so I reported him to my management at Brookhaven. I told DOE that I had been too difficult a case for him. If he ever reported to DOE on the content of our sessions, I never heard about it.

I went back to Dr. Buono who referred me to Dr. Edwin Sause. He and I clicked immediately. It was good to have someone to talk to, but after my prior experience on the snoozing analyst's couch anything would have been an improvement.

The panic attacks and nightmares continued, even on the meds. Sometimes there were two in a day; some days there were literally dozens in a row. I would come out of it and try to catch some sleep before the next one hit. There was very little uninterrupted sleep.

I sold my boat, a 35-foot cabin cruiser I had named "Susie Q," afraid of what might happen when I was piloting her. It's hard enough coming through the channel when you're sober and the weather's good; what would happen if I had a panic attack when I was close to other boats?

I'd never even heard of PTSD before I was diagnosed with it, but the term refers to severe psychological consequences of exposure to events someone finds highly traumatic, and his usual psychological defenses aren't able to cope with them. For most people, the effects of traumatic events tend to subside after several months, but I had never had the time to process what I had seen; there had been too much work to do immediately after 9/11.

And even if I had had the time, I might not have talked about what happened, even with Sue. I was from a military background and a traditional family. It's not about being stoic or brave; men keep their suffering to themselves and don't burden their families with their problems. Most vets are the same way; we don't get together and talk about our feelings; we do what we're required to do and keep our mouths shut. Even to this very day, I still find it hard to believe, let alone admit, that I have this condition. I refuse to believe that I cannot maintain control, even after having lived with this for several years. People still amaze me with stories like, "Do you remember you had that attack at Christmas time?" *Hell, no, I don't remember! That's what one part of the problem is.*

I met with the woman from our Chicago office at Brookhaven to discuss my security clearance. I wanted to keep my clearance, of course, and they had every right to examine me, given that I was working in potentially volatile and even possibly catastrophic scenarios. That was no place for someone experiencing panic attacks. That was the reason why I took myself out of that position for a short rest.

But that wasn't what our conversation was about.

"It's come to our attention that you have a problem with alcohol," were the first words out of her mouth.

"Where in the world did that come from?" I demanded to know.

"We've been documenting it for some time," she replied.

"I've been diagnosed with Post Traumatic Stress Disorder," I reminded her. "If I drink it's because I can't sleep at night."

"I don't know about that, but the alcoholism is a serious threat to your security clearance," she said.

"If you've been documenting like you say, and you're concerned that it's a serious problem, why did you wait until now to bring it up?"

It was my first jolt of realization that DOE was not going to help me. Not only did they not wish to recognize the PTSD diagnosis, they were building a case for my dismissal based on the charge that I was an alcoholic.

"I'd like to see the evidence you've been documenting," I demanded, but I didn't lose my temper. I knew they would hold that against me, so it was in my best interest, even though I was furious, to remain under control.

She ignored my demand. To this day no documented evidence of my alcohol abuse was ever produced, incidentally. Nor has the government explained to me in writing, as required by federal regulations, as to why they suspended my security clearance.

"We want you to visit another psychiatrist for an evaluation," she told me. "He's in Albany. Take the day, stay over on our dime, and we'll get a professional opinion on your case."

"I'm being set up," I told Sue when I got home. DOE wasn't interested in my problems, only in building a case against me so they could make me go away. I was a top performer, dedicated and uncomplaining, but now that I was suffering they regarded me as a nuisance, and I sensed they were going to say whatever was necessary to make me disappear.

The psychiatrist in Albany spent an hour with me. It seemed predetermined before I ever walked through the door. How much of a diagnosis can a psychiatrist make in less than an hour?

His verdict: I was a security risk.

"I would rather give up my security clearance than have you take it away," I told my boss. I knew at that point that the decision was an inevitability. They were going to find one reason or another to be rid of me.

Beginning with the back injury, through my initial complaints, on to my diagnosis and the lousy sleepy psychologist they'd sent me to, the response to my growing problems had been poorly handled. Now they were going to ignore the PTSD diagnosis, accuse me of being an alcoholic and a security risk, and find a reason to terminate me, and possibly deny me benefits.

They wanted me to go away as fast as possible with as little embarrassment to them as possible. I felt that they thought it would have been better for them had I died instead because it would not show up on their data as a work-related lost-time incident. What options did I have?

Unknown to me at the time and not coincidentally, the Bush administration was beginning its assault on Iraq War veterans by using operatives (who are also psychiatrists) of the American Enterprise Institute (AEI) to attack diagnoses of PTSD and disparage the veterans afflicted with the disorder as "malingerers," stating that combat damaged veterans are trying to game the system to bilk the taxpayers out of their money.

Compensating troops properly is only part of the idea behind the PTSD denials; the horror and mismanagement of the Iraq War are obscured by blaming the veterans. According to the administration, the high incidence rate of PTSD among veterans is caused by personal defects and greed.

Me? I was just a drunk who couldn't be trusted with all the responsibility they had— until I complained about being ill— completely trusted me with, including the personal security and safety of the President of the United States.

CHAPTER 32

I returned from my thirty days' prescribed bed rest no better rested and no happier with my situation at DOE.

On one hand, being home for thirty days had given me a reprieve from the relentless NEST schedule, and the drugs had slowed the panic attacks. But even though I hadn't slept soundly during the preceding four years, I still couldn't sleep now that I had the opportunity. Every night I would fight to relax and finally nod off around three or four in the morning for a few hours.

Something still wasn't right with me besides the lack of sleep. It's hard to describe, but it was similar to the sensation you have when you're looking for something important, like your wallet. You look where it ought to be and it's not there. You look where it might be and it's not there. You look everywhere you can think of, even the illogical places, and you still can't find it, and all the while your frustration is mounting.

That's how I felt every minute of every day, with one difference: I had no idea what I was looking for, and I had no idea where to find this unnamed thing. And the longer I felt the need to locate this unnamed thing the more the anxiety was compounded.

In retrospect I think it was guilt that plagued me, the nagging feeling that I was letting my team down and not fulfilling my obligation to serve my country. There are lunatics out there with bombs, and I'm lying in bed! This isn't what I signed up for!

The panic attacks also left me feeling uneasy and guilty, because I had no memory of them. I never had nor do I have now any recollection of them. I do remember once in the hospital the nurses calling the doctor and reporting an emergency regarding my situation. They said I had a seizure and that my eyes had rolled back in my head.

I thought they were nuts because I didn't remember feeling a thing. But that was the way it was when I had attacks. I just don't remember. I still sometimes have them, again with no memory. Sue tells me my whole body convulses while I'm lying down or napping, and when I wake up it's as though it never happened.

I didn't know it or understand it at the time. The notion of panic attacks made no sense to me. It still doesn't even to this day.

Going back to work didn't help. Management at Brookhaven did everything in its power to make me even more anxious. They took my badge and replaced it with one that indicated that I didn't have a security clearance. They took away my office and put me in one right outside the manager's office, a fishbowl where everyone could see my every movement. They gave me no work to do, and I don't mean they gave me no meaningful work or no work I enjoyed doing: I mean absolutely zero. And they clearly indicated to the support staff that I had been relegated to outsider status, so virtually no one would talk to me, and when they had to in the normal course of business they were stiff.

My five team members remained conversational; we were a close group, and I think they understood that I had removed myself from the team to protect them, and the public. They understood I was all about the job, and maintaining our safety and integrity. But even they were cautious about being seen talking to me.

In short time I had gone from being DOE's star at Brookhaven to being an outcast, almost overnight and for no other reason than I had asked for help for a problem I didn't really understand.

Meanwhile, DOE couldn't find anyone willing to shoulder my

load with the NEST team, so they got a part-time replacement, an agent who lived in Idaho who was willing to work occasionally out of Brookhaven because he had family in the area, and the NEST assignments my former team couldn't handle were covered by a team based in the DC area.

I wasn't allowed to ask about NEST or RAP assignments, or answer questions about them. I wasn't officially told what was happening with those assignments because I had been deemed a "security risk." In fact, I was still being told my time away was considered AWOL because the doctors hadn't sufficiently documented what was wrong with me.

I still wasn't sure what was wrong with me, either. It's hard to explain to others an anxiety you can't identify and panic attacks you can't remember.

I felt like I had become a leper at Brookhaven, but rather than treat the leper DOE opted to make me feel like an outcast.

The two people closest to me in the hierarchy of the organization were the worst to deal with. One, being officious and distrustful in general, made certain I felt like an outcast and made certain everyone understood that ignoring me was the unofficial protocol. On the other side was my assistant, whose principal duty was to keep the team and equipment in a state of perpetual readiness, but instead she always seemed to be looking for the spotlight, which I had no use for, and she knew it.

One day she said to me, "I know we've had our differences in the past, but I'd like to bury the hatchet."

I agreed, not realizing she was burying her hatchet in my back, going to my management with false reports about my personal behavior, I didn't realize that anything I did on my own time would be used to build a case against me, mostly because while I was hurt by DOE's treatment of me, I still couldn't believe they would abandon me.

Of course I was aware that even though we at DOE were ostensibly in the business of protecting the country, developing weapons and defenses and strategies, we were still a bureaucracy, and one that was badly run at that. In retrospect, DOE was a model for how *not* to run a management system, because the system was ripe for abuse and some people couldn't resist the temptation to stick their hand in the cookie jar.

With most of our work done by contractors there was a great deal of abuse built into the system, primarily because loyalty was paid for rather than earned. People like me worked for the federal government and considered serving and protecting the country a sacred duty. For a lot of DOE contractor employees, working for the DOE was just a *job*.

And it was a job where the contractors determined how much something would cost and how long it would take them to do the job. As a bonus they could quit at any time without repercussion.

Our next-generation particle accelerator was a good example. Bids came in for the job, and as soon as the contract was awarded the cost started going up. Miscalculations and errors added to the cost, deadlines were missed, and no one was penalized. Had the contractor dropped the project without finishing, as often happened, DOE would simply start the process over without attempting to recoup any of the expended funds.

That's a bad system, but from what's said about federal contracting in general it appears to be the industry norm.

There were also the contractors who felt empowered doing work for the federal government. It didn't necessarily make them better workers, but it gave them an air of authority.

We'd meet with a state agency like DEP or OEM to explain a procedure, and I'd overhear one of our contractors promising that we'd return to provide training, and I'm thinking, *He's not authorized to promise any such thing, and he's indemnified against legal action if anything goes wrong, so I'm the guy they'll come after.*

I'd estimate that ninety-five percent of the contractors were loyal and did a good job. But that five percent who did abuse the system abused the hell out of it.

But I was only peripherally aware of what was going on at this point. I'd been removed from the process as punishment for seeking help. At this point I think they were hoping I'd be ashamed of my loss of privilege and quit, but I was focusing my energies on getting through the day, not on what I was going to do next.

I'd rise every morning for work, exhausted and anxious, sit at my desk for eight hours surfing the Internet (a new experience for me, since I hadn't had the time to do anything more in the past with my computer than send reports and e-mails) and come home even more anxious and angry than I was when I left. Then after dinner with Sue I'd go to the VFW and have a few drinks with my buddies, come home and try to go to sleep only to spend hours tossing and turning and hoping this would be the night I finally got a good night's sleep.

Finally, after ignoring me for months, one of my managers accosted me. "All you're doing is screwing yourself over," he advised me. "All you're doing with this restricted duty designation is losing your security clearance."

"So?" I replied. "I've got nothing to do and you've already taken away my security clearance. I've asked you for help and I didn't get any. You send me letters saying I'm AWOL. I don't know what I did that was so wrong. I came to you with my problems, you didn't come to me, and now you're treating me like I did something wrong."

He didn't respond to this. He just walked away.

Christmas was even more stressful, as if that was possible. I'd spent the previous several Christmases in a state of constant alertness, looking for terrorists like the ones who had attacked the Twin Towers, and this year I was sitting at a desk inside my fishbowl with nothing to do. The frustration inside me was escalating, the anxious sense that I was searching relentlessly for something that was indefinable gripped me.

I should have enjoyed being home with my family for Christmas instead of running around the northeast with my team, but I couldn't enjoy it. I couldn't enjoy anything. There was no refuge from the suffocating anxiety and feeling that something inside me wasn't right.

It was the first week of January when I walked up to Sue, who was standing in the kitchen. I don't know what finally prompted it, but the cumulative physical and psychological effects of the previous four years had finally worn me out completely.

"Sue, I need you to take me to the hospital," I said.

But her memories of what happened in those days are clearer than mine.

CHAPTER 33

Sue Centore, Steve's wife, explains what happened:
In early January, I took the opportunity to discuss with Steve whenever he seemed a bit coherent that we may need to get him professional care at a hospital of some sort. I let him process this, and when he was ready he came to me and said he wanted to get to a hospital, that it was time.

I had finally convinced him that the situation was dire. I immediately started calling local hospitals, but every facility said the same thing: they couldn't take someone with both severe PTSD and an alcohol issue. I cried myself to sleep night after night as every call resulted in a dead end.

After four years of this crisis building we'd hit a dead end.

When the panic attacks first hit it was like a switch had been flipped in Steve's brain. I noticed that two months prior he had become acutely aware that people were dying all around him. Each nightly news program mentioning rescue workers who were sick or dying were captured in detail and recounted in subsequent conversations. Then came the abrupt passing

133

of a dear friend of ours, Delores Bigrow, who was struck and killed by a car while taking an early evening stroll in her neighborhood in broad daylight.

We stayed by her husband John's side the first night or so until relatives could arrive, so were immersed in the darkness of the moment. After the first day staying with John, I knew I had to relieve Steve of his duties there because he had become hypersensitive to death. I let him go home while I stayed with John for another night.

Delores, or De as she was often called, was about the friendliest farm girl you'd ever want to meet. She was just a pure and true, no-bones-about-it kind of a person who always thought of everyone else before herself, constantly doing special things for others, and always made us laugh with her special way of poking a little fun at the husband she loved so much. Their love was sweet and pure and fun, and so out of place in New York, and she was now gone, and I knew her passing left a permanent impression on Steve, as much as a branding iron leaves a mark on a steer. In a moment, she was gone. There was no sense to it…it didn't fit neatly into the brain of anyone. But in Steve's brain there was a whole other level of trauma.

It makes perfect sense to me in retrospect…the path that led Steve to his physical and mental meltdown. Ever since he worked at Ground Zero he experienced and accumulated more and more physical anomalies. Finally in 2005, he began sensing something was much more wrong in his body than the individual ailments; he also sensed something was very wrong in his mind.

From the first time he came home from Ground Zero (barely just for a day, if that) and every subsequent time (which also amounted to one day, if that), he was completely exhausted and spent all his time trying to sleep on the couch. He could not reconnect with us at home (me and his youngest son, Steven, then fifteen years old). For one thing, he did not want to speak of what he had seen, but even in the hour or two of interaction we might have had while he was home each time, his phone would constantly be ringing with one crisis or another that the various agencies and entities needed him to resolve. Whether it was dealing with the authorities on possible radiation sources, or coordinating coverage of radiation teams coming in from all over the country, he could not rest.

I hoped it would end with the end of his four months at Ground Zero but in fact it continued for about another three and a half years from then. Therein lay the problem. Steve's RAP job somehow morphed into this high-profile NEST assignment with tremendous responsibility. Somehow he became every agency's go-to guy in all matters related to radiation detection training and covert operations. He was constantly away from home, and when he was at home, he spent most of his time on the phone, usually followed by a packing of the bags. Then he was off again.

Steve felt a slave to the phone and felt sometimes as though he had ten bosses. People of significant authority from city government to state agencies to the military to federal government called upon him directly at all hours of the day and night, and he was compelled to jump up and deliver.

This led to a complete inability for him to devote any time to himself, and to give any attention at all to the increasing health concerns…he actually felt it dishonorable to complain of any ailments, especially when there was so much important work to be done.

Steve barely managed one doctor appointment within the first year, which he had to fit in because his blood pressure went through the roof within the first couple months after 9/11, and he probably didn't make it to another appointment until almost two years after the first one. He couldn't schedule appointments because he was gone all the time and could expect to continue to be gone all the time anytime in the foreseeable future.

Whenever he did make doctors' appointments, one by one he had to cancel them all. DOE kept promising they would get him some additional support to ease the workload, but the promises were empty and produced nothing, and the demands on him just kept increasing.

Worst of all, Steve really held on to the hope that help was coming. He believed in them…he really needed to believe in them. At some point, it became the one thing that he hung on to, that the government would be there to help him when the crisis, or the never ending series of crises, finally passed.

He was physically and mentally stretched and exhausted. He was keeping a demanding pace and doing so many covert ops runs that even a twenty-year-old would have trouble keeping up. And his body was taking the toll.

CHAPTER 34

*A*fter a few years of that pace heading the NEST team, Steve started looking much older than his years. He continued to have sleep problems, high blood pressure, sleep apnea, strange skin rashes, increased breathing issues, troubles with uncontrolled bleeding, nightmares, and constant bloody noses. Aside from a brief one-week getaway to Aruba in July, 2003 for our honeymoon, Steve had not been able to take a vacation or get the comp time that had been accumulating since 9/11.

When he did try to take some time, it was spent at home, slaving to the phones for hours every day, and again, often ending in an unplanned run out the door. We barely were able to make time for our wedding, an event that we saw as necessary as Steve was then constantly in harm's way on covert ops, and he still had a teenager at home whose safety and welfare he was concerned about.

Even as we returned from that Aruba trip, Steve had to repack his bags and was gone immediately for another three weeks on the job.

The next summer, Steve coughed all summer long, to the point where he broke a blood vessel in his chest that left a large bruise that stayed with *him for a long time. He had no time to get to a doctor about it, but eventually had to as it created a lump on his breast for which he ultimately had to have a mammogram done to rule out some kind of cancer.*

When his schedule started to let up a little in 2005, Steve began trying to take vacation time and comp time accumulated over the years since 9/11, which met with great resistance from the Brookhaven DOE office. They hadn't seen much of him in the previous four years, and seemed to resent him taking the time due him. Yet at the same time, the payroll system wouldn't allow for a monetary reimbursement for the time due, so he could either throw away months and months of time due him or try to take some of it.

Steve started taking time in 2005, which began with a long-awaited trip to the U.K. to visit with friends. We took two and a half weeks, and upon our return Steve again packed his bags and was gone the next day to Washington, DC…only he never made it there.

While dragging his luggage through Penn Station to catch an Amtrak train, something in his back popped and he was in excruciating pain, enough so that he turned around and caught the local train back home. When I came home from work, he was curled up in a ball on the kitchen floor, literally crying in pain. An X-ray showed herniated discs in his lower back, for which they initially prescribed painkillers with a recommendation for a follow-up visit to determine the next step.

The painkillers, however, were too extreme for Steve and caused him to hallucinate, and he couldn't function at work as they left him too doped up. He had to stop taking them after the first day or two, which left him to simply suffer with the pain. He continued that entire week in agonizing pain, and then needed to return to work, which meant he couldn't take any painkillers at all, so he simply worked and dealt with the pain without any medication. Of course, he couldn't really do his job with the pain, as he almost always had to carry heavy bags wherever he went.

He wasn't a complainer, but he knew he couldn't survive at work under the circumstances. But when he asked the Brookhaven DOE office for some time off, which he very desperately needed, he got flack. After all this time, after four years operating the NEST team, there still wasn't enough manpower to enable Steve to take some time off.

Attempts to obtain Workman's Compensation for this injury met with failure. He was busting his ass for this organization, for this government, and they wouldn't even consider compensating him for this injury. After jumping from Coast Guard boats in open water, to shouldering heavy radiation detection gear on foot for an untold number of covert detection operations, getting mugged several times in New York City on the job, and somehow they deemed this injury as not being work-related?

He was in pain because of the demands of this job and he had to live with the insult that his own employer could care less about his problems. In fact, the only attention they paid him was to bust his chops about calling in sick with e-mails versus telephone calls, putting him on record as being AWOL even when he could produce medical notes regarding his ailments.

The treatment by Steve's employer was beating him down psychologically. At a time when he should have been able to relax just a little bit and maybe recuperate from four intensive years of labor, he instead was starting to feel the physical backlash of the years of pushing his body and his mind beyond its limits, and the Brookhaven office had little understanding or compassion for his situation.

The inability for Steve to effectively manage his pain left him to turn to drinking alcohol in order to go to sleep, only when he finally went to sleep he was having very vivid nightmares, visions seemingly pent up and accumulated from 9/11, where he'd see the body parts strewn around the pile. He was in an impossibly crazy situation of desperately needing to sleep, yet not being able to, either from back pain or from the nightmares. It's not a surprise that the drinking became a problem, because eventually it was the only way he could get any rest.

Sensing he was really pushing himself too hard, he tried to take time off whenever he could, and asked others in the local DOE office to stand in for him, but his superiors were not pleased with that solution. They wanted him to continue that insane pace, even though nobody at Brookhaven truly understood what Steve had been handling for the past four years, or how hard the schedule was on him. They seemed annoyed by his various complaints of not feeling right and his requests that DOE needed to train people who were capable of relieving him of at least part of his workload. They didn't seem to care and very clearly didn't even believe he was ill at all.

It was during this time that we lost of our friend, Delores, which tore him down some more. And then, finally, the straw that snapped in Steve's mind came in the evening news report in August, 2005 that a couple more rescue workers had succumbed to their illnesses from working at Ground Zero.

Steve was distraught that night with the passing of more people like him, first responders who were at Ground Zero for far too long. With their death, he saw his own death coming. He had been feeling it in his body and now he was beginning to feel it psychologically; he was finally beginning to pay some attention to the various health problems he'd been experiencing since 2001 and was realizing how much his health had deteriorated.

Steve started having panic attacks overnight after that news broadcast about the fallen rescue workers. I hadn't slept in the same bedroom with him since 2001 due to his newly acquired sleep apnea problem and his inability to sleep through the night, not to mention his need to have all the lights on in the room through the night; he was never home much anymore anyway, so there didn't seem any point in even trying anymore.

But this night I heard his cries from down the hall and came running to him, as he cried in terror over things I couldn't calm him down from, as if he were in the midst of a battle seeing unspeakable horrors right before his eyes—the terror in his eyes and tenseness of his body frightened me, and with tears welling up in my own eyes, I tried to talk him down from the horror.

He was scared to death of demons I couldn't see, and thus began almost a solid week of entirely sleepless nights for us both as the cycle continued with me trying to rest lightly down the hall in between a constant onslaught of severe post traumatic stress episodes that called me to attention, running down the hall to his rescue.

I stayed home from work for several days, spending every moment at Steve's side, running through this insane cycle that didn't let up even during the day. He'd get a fearful look in his eyes, then go blank. He knew it was coming and he'd call to me, but all I could do was hold him until it passed. There was no stopping the attacks. I was exhausted and he was exhausted and after several long, long days, he was so exhausted that he finally managed to sleep for an hour here or there during the days.

He shifted to a cycle of catching these daytime hour naps, and then staying up all night for fear of falling asleep and falling victim to the nightmares and demons awaiting him when his eyes closed.

At some point, I attempted to return to work while he attempted to sleep during the days, but I spent all my time calling him and checking on him, and became panicky when I couldn't get hold of him. I never slept through the night from then on and instead only rested at night, waiting for him to call to me.

He also began to get confused easily and seemed to have lapses in memory. And he never remembered the panic attacks. When I would ask him about 9/11, what it was that was tormenting him, all he could say was, "You don't know what it's like." Which was true; I had no frame of reference. He couldn't relate to normal people, and the only people he'd be able to relate to were others who were there.

I learned to keep things away from him that might trigger the attacks. Anything about death might do it. We were at my brother's house and there was a pamphlet on the coffee table for an exhibit in New York City called "Bones," featuring dissected human bodies. I hid it. Another time we were visiting his son's house for Christmas and someone put on the movie "Sin City," which was very graphic in its violence, and I could see Steve start to go to that place, like his brain was trying to process what he was seeing. He'd look at me the way a dog does when it's curious, with his head tilted and his eyes far away, and I would know that he was going to a dark place, that the demons were lurking just around the corner.

I know that if he had never gone to Ground Zero he wouldn't have had the physical or psychological problems he developed. But as bad as he was physically, as much as the demons tormented him and his physical health deteriorated and the alcohol use exacerbated all of his problems, the final straw was DOE's refusal to acknowledge his problems. It wasn't as though he blamed his government, after all, for what he endured and how he had been afflicted. He just wanted their help, and they not only refused to assist him, they blamed him for his problems.

Despite everything he remained loyal and stoic and uncomplaining until they gave him no options. It was their betrayal, their refusal to help and their blaming him that ultimately broke his spirit and brought what remained of what his life had been crashing to the ground.

CHAPTER 35

Steve attempted to work from home and take sick or vacation time over the next few weeks, but he was still catching flack from the Brookhaven management. They were meticulously black and white about the method Steve would use to call in sick or vacation time, and continued to threaten him with citing him as AWOL. On the day I hand delivered a note from Steve's family doctor, on Sept. 12, 2005, stating that he needed one month leave of absence effective immediately, they sent a certified letter which we received the next day stating he was AWOL until such time as he filled out and returned additional signed documents from both him and his doctor explaining why he was sick and when the sickness would end…as if anyone could neatly explain what his ailments were and when they would end.

I recalled that when Steve made his first visit to his family doctor shortly after his four months at Ground Zero, and his blood pressure was dangerously high, his doctor said, "Steve, you need to quit this job. Do you have to continue with this work? This work is gonna kill you." The doctor would repeat these same words on each subsequent visit, urging Steve each and every time to quit the job or die early from the physical impact it was making on him, from the stress alone. Now that prognosis seemed to be coming true.

So, for the first two weeks of what was supposed to be an immediate month of downtime, Steve spent his time trying to put together the necessary paperwork for DOE, and tried to get his doctor to drop everything and write an additional letter for DOE management to explain a mental and physical condition he didn't yet understand. Brookhaven harassed him daily about being AWOL until this paperwork was done.

The term struck Steve's nerve. How the hell did they get off using a term for him representing the most dishonorable thing military personnel could do? No one among his managers had ever served in the military. After Steve's sacrifices and burdens in the Navy (serving an extended tour of six years, being exposed to asbestos and radiation; being gone so much that his wife walked out on him and left him to raise three very young babies/children by himself while still enlisted), after serving as an active officer in the local VFW, and most recently sacrificing absolutely everything (his relationship with me and with his youngest son who really needed him at this time, and now sacrificing his own mental and physical health), and all his management could do was turn a deaf ear and bust his chops.

The icing on the cake is that in this same timeframe that Steve was supposed to be taking a break from the stress of the job, the local DOE office arranged a surprise two-hour audio-taped meeting of a Chicago DOE investigator that was presented innocently as an unofficial talk. It was in fact an interrogation that apparently was focused on trying to prove Steve was simply a drunk and stripping him of his security clearance.

Steve was never the same after that. He plunged deeper into the depths of his own private hell after this incident. DOE was back-stabbing him and stripping him of his dignity and was as cold and callous as I'd ever witnessed people being. I was dumfounded by their actions. I was crushed and angry at the same time. While I tried to hold the house of cards together that was now my husband's life and as I tried to keep from losing my own job due to all the attention I had to pay to Steve, I now had to jump through hoops trying to deal with DOE demands so Steve would not lose his job while I tried to find medical and mental help for him.

The DOE office was of no help as they were focused on a witch hunt to strip him of his clearance. Their help was to send him to an EAP (Employee Assistance Program) counselor who fell asleep on Steve on his second visit, and then declared he couldn't help Steve. Then they set up some interview with a government psychiatrist up in Albany, N.Y., seemingly to decide whether or not he could keep his clearance. Steve had nothing to hide and agreed to this meeting, even though it was a difficult trip to make as I had to drive him everywhere by now. He was having severe panic attacks that left it too dangerous for him to drive so I had to take more and more time from work to get him to doctors' appointments and things like this six hour drive each way to Albany.

We drove there, and Steve met with this guy for one hour who didn't even have Steven's file or any paperwork pertaining to Steve. It was a complete waste of time and we knew it immediately when we got there, that it was nothing more than a formality and that somebody somewhere had likely already made some decision about Steve's clearance, independent of this psychiatric evaluation.

After this charade, Steve requested several times for DOE to state the status of his clearance and whether or not it was officially stripped from him; if so, what was the reason? They never did respond to that inquiry, even to this day.

So the "month off" became the month-long parade of overt harassment by DOE. They pounded their salt directly into the already open meat of the wound. He would spend October, November and December in deep turmoil. He spent more and more time on the couch, unable to pick himself up, focused on nothing but the betrayal by DOE and his government and unable to understand what he had done to deserve it. He was inconsolable, but it wasn't anger he felt (I was the one who had the corner on that market), it was utter disbelief, sorrow, and dismay, as if his own mother had driven a knife into his belly and he couldn't comprehend why.

He wailed and wept often for hours on end, rocking himself, trying to console his own soul. And I spent most of my time at his side, crying along with him…crying for him because his emotion was so raw and it ripped me apart to see him like this…crying for me because I, too, felt lost, let down, and alone. Aside from a few phone calls to only certain family members, I couldn't share this all with anyone…I was barely managing the crazy daily cycle of trying to keep showing up at work myself, trying to keep tabs on

Steve through the day, rushing home when he didn't sound right or I couldn't get in touch with him, barely cat napping through the night as I snapped to attention every time he cried out, talking him down from countless increasing panic attacks.

I often found him in the kitchen or in the middle of the driveway in his underwear or pajamas staring off into space in a catatonic state, his arm shaking at his side in a strange steady pace; I could stand right before him and he couldn't see me at all.

The federal medical monitoring program that was supposed to be Steve's outlet for reporting his conditions from working at Ground Zero was a big letdown. They offered no help at all. I spent any free time I had trying to research where I could get help for his PTSD. I couldn't find anything. The Veterans Administration was my first hope as they certainly would have experience with PTSD, but they turned us away since Steve made too much money. I didn't want to send him to a psychiatric hospital because they were too depressing and they didn't have a good program for PTSD. Mount Sinai hospital in New York City couldn't help because Steve was a federal employee and they had no advice on programs for Ground Zero workers suffering from PTSD.

Despite my best efforts I wasn't able to manage the situation and he had begun drinking very heavily to escape his mental and physical pain.

By the time Christmas 2005 came, Steven Jr. had come to visit from college, and I drove us all down to Maryland to visit with Steve's son Chuck, his wife Frankie, and our new grandson Dante. Photos of Steve from that time show how yellow his skin was. He looked thin and very ill. He had several panic attacks while there...one at the neighbor's house while in the bathroom, one while watching the first five minutes of "Sin City." I was constantly shifting conversations mid-stream with others who might speak inadvertently of a sick or dying friend or family member, or of an accident they'd seen, or shielding him from graphic images.

I was angry and distraught in this period of time, and I was in this alone. Nobody could help Steve, so nobody was of any help to me and I felt the desperation of that reality. Steve tried to show up periodically to work in those months on what he determined to be his better days and remained home on the worst of them. I never knew which day was which. By December every day was a bad day, and although I thought Steve was reporting to management when he was not coming in to work, I hadn't realized how detached he had become that month. At some point, I had to step in and report his absences for him to DOE management. I resented their lack of humanity as they enforced protocol.

The terrorists may have caused the 9/11 disaster, but DOE left Steve standing alone to deal with the real heat of the job and couldn't provide even minimal support that might have saved him from this breakdown. They turned their backs on this one guy who really cared about his job and his duty to his government and country. To this day, the thought of them still makes my stomach turn.

By the end of December 2005, Steve's physical health was severely compromised. He had full-blown panic attacks regularly with full body tremors that jolted him as if he were being electrocuted. I would lie next to him holding him and trying to comfort him. He was delirious when he came out of them, only to utter words about his government betraying him before he slipped into the next one.

The nightmares were no longer reserved for nighttime and sleeping...they were here in pure daylight as though his life were his battlefield. Steve became more and more crushed as my attempts to help him all failed. We both became desperate and cried in each other's arms uncontrollably as there was nobody who would help us. We just wanted to get him into someone's care, but nobody would take us.

With no other options, I had to stretch or hide the truth to get him into any facility I could. I no longer presented him as a dual problem patient, and I still had trouble getting him immediately into a facility as nobody had any beds available. I was told we'd have to wait days or a week or so. I didn't have that sort of time. I had a man who was on the edge of his sanity, who was agreeing to check in somewhere for help, and I couldn't find him a damned bed.

Finally, someone tipped me off to the fact that if Steve were suicidal, I could bring him to a hospital emergency room and they would have to take him in. It was no stretch to say that Steve was suicidal because he at times wished he were dead and told me so. He was drinking heavily enough to kill himself and I felt he was in a way committing suicide with that bottle.

I wanted to get him to Mather Hospital in Port Jefferson, because they had a psychiatric unit and I figured that was the best option, because I was certain he needed medical care as strongly as the psychiatric care.

Besides, although they, too, didn't have a dual program (psychiatric and alcohol), I knew technically they had the capacity.

I packed a bag and tried to get him up from the couch, but then he decided he didn't want to go. I broke down at this point, and disappeared into a room and wailed uncontrollably for fifteen minutes or so. I'd felt that I'd reached the end, that I'd lost the battle, and that Steve would die if I didn't get him to the hospital immediately.

After pulling myself together, I thought to call my brother Ken to come and help me. With Ken and my sister-in-law, Marie at the house, they might be able to talk Steve into going to the hospital. I needed to get him to Port Jefferson, a thirty-plus minute ride from the house, so a local ambulance was not an option. Ken and Marie showed up, and with just a little coaxing, they were able to convince Steve to go to the hospital.

He didn't go down entirely without a fight, though; as he insisted on stopping at a gas station to buy a quart of beer on the way to the hospital. It became a condition of his following through on the plan, so he got his way.

CHAPTER 36

When they tested Steve's vitals and blood in the emergency room, after remarking on the obvious levels of alcohol in his blood, they immediately admitted him to the medical facilities because his over-all blood counts were so severely screwed up.

He spent five days in the regular medical unit, where they tried to get his blood counts under control, and they gave him meds for alcohol withdrawal. In the meantime, a CAT scan showed a twenty percent shrinkage of his brain.

With each day in the hospital Steve seemed to be getting worse. He couldn't walk straight, but instead leaned on the hallway walls with his right shoulder and pretty much slid his way down the hall. At that point, they said there was not much that could be done for him and that the damage to his brain might be permanent. They transferred him to the psychiatric center at my request (they were otherwise intending to release him), because I insisted he needed a full psychiatric evaluation.

Steve couldn't walk on his own in the psychiatric unit and wasn't able to be involved in any of their normal daily programs. He was continuing *with some other narcotic-based medication to transition off of the initial meds they gave him for the alcohol withdrawal, but despite the prescribed treatment each day he was obviously worse than the previous.*

I traveled forty minutes every day from work to see Steve and stayed round-the-clock initially against regular hospital rules because he was doing so poorly, and nobody could explain why. The worst situation was when I showed up and he had wet the bed and was lying in the wet sheets. He couldn't speak and could only lift his arm a couple of inches from his side. He tried to communicate with his eyes and with grunting, but it took me at least a half hour to figure out he was wet. I didn't know what had happened and the staff didn't have any answers for it. I think it was on a weekend so there were several changes in staff, and I don't think any one person was responsible for watching him, and unsupervised his rapid deterioration went unnoticed.

I insisted they stop one of the new medicines that I surmised was the immediate culprit. They wouldn't let me stay the night, but swore to me they'd stop the meds and that I could call first thing in the morning to follow up. I left late that night, so I could be sure the night nurse wouldn't give him any meds and I returned first thing in the morning before regular visiting hours.

I was oblivious to my condition and everything going on around me, but the nurses later told me the doctor advised them that night, "Don't get too attached to this one. He won't make it through the weekend."

But I made it through the weekend after all. While I was in the comatose state, I had an out-of-body experience. I was looking down on myself in bed, and all these little multi-colored lights surrounded me, and I could see that they were sucking me out of my body. And I was thinking of the movie *Poltergeist*, but instead of going into the light I was thinking, *No, don't go into the light.*

I wasn't comforted by the idea of dying, I wanted to fight it. And I struggled to wake up, to get back inside my body, and when I finally forced myself to consciousness I was still there, but I had emptied my bowels into my bed.

Steve had soiled himself throughout the night, and they had to diaper and change him constantly.

I firmly believe if I hadn't insisted they stop the meds that he would shortly have died from an overdose. Nobody ever confirmed or validated my suspicion (Why would they, right?), but I speculated that his body wasn't filtering out the narcotic medication they were giving him so each additional dosage was accumulating, and eventually he reached a point where he was overdosing. They had to reintroduce a smaller dosage of the medication the next day and subsequent days after to wean him off of the drug, and gradually the man they had taken for dead slowly came back to life.

After about two weeks at the hospital they were ready to release him with a list of meds and recommendations for continued psychiatric counseling. I convinced Steve to also seek alcohol counseling as he obviously could not continue drinking with a damaged brain and a new medication regimen, and that he really needed to get to the bottom of the psychological issues that had turned him to the bottle in the first place. He agreed and we told them to include it as part of the release plan.

I did my research and was interested in a facility near our home that had a program for those with mental disorder issues that also provided alcohol counseling, which I saw as the best fit we could manage. As it turned out, once we were there we realized they didn't actually do much for treating mental illness, but the general alcohol counseling programs were at least an avenue for Steve to start talking about the things that were tormenting him, and avoiding alcohol as a crutch to get him through the pain helped him to focus on what was really wrong.

The center did have a problem with taking in someone whose blood counts were still so screwed up, and he almost was not allowed in, but they agreed to let him in as long as he had blood drawn each day to recheck his counts. We were so grateful for the chance to have gotten him in there…it was a bridge to Steve regaining his sanity.

He hated it there most of the time, and I hated him being away for so long as I slept in this house filled with Steve's demons, all alone with my own thoughts, but as unpleasant as it was it honestly served us both well.

He eventually was able to sleep at night and I eventually was able to as well, which was an amazing development all by itself, given the previous months of sleeplessness.

After Steve finally came back home to me, we began the next series of challenges. While he was making progress in trying to piece back together his mind, physically he was getting worse. His blood counts remained out *of whack. He went to several specialists who were bouncing back and forth between a bad gallbladder or a bad liver. They couldn't do exploratory surgery, though, because Steve had an existing condition of uncontrollable bleeding, so they relied on medications to get things under control.*

In June 2006, Steve had some kind of attack while my mom was visiting. He was unable to lift himself from the bed and was becoming noticeably confused and delirious, and it seemed he would pass out entirely…it was frightening and incredibly upsetting to me but even in his confusion, Steve didn't want to worry me, and tried to spare me being upset by calling my mom aside to confide in her that he needed an ambulance.

He was rushed to the hospital where they found his ammonia levels were out of whack. He stayed for about a week there before being released. In August 2006, he was sent to the hospital straight from the hematologist appointment he had because his platelets were unbalanced, for which he was admitted to the hospital yet again.

It seemed that we floundered that year and were wasting valuable time without any real answers as to what else was wrong with Steve. He was having more and more trouble getting around, was getting incredibly winded and was having a real problem with water retention. Steroids he was placed on in the summer of 2006 seemed to make his overall health worse as he had a hard time coming off them.

Additional physical ailments had been manifesting themselves in my body: problems with my liver, kidneys and bone marrow and no gallbladder function. I was given Prednisone, a steroid that made me feel like Superman, with the hope that the steroid would get my organs back to working at normal capacity, which they did, at least initially. But when they weaned me off Prednisone the withdrawal made me feel like I was going to die. I felt that pain all the way down in my bones. After about a month of intense pain, it went away.

I worked out an arrangement where I could still work for DOE, mostly at home. They eventually moved me from the fishbowl to a desk in the back, but I was still doing bullshit work, and there was no benefit in me actually being there. Working from home made the arrangement easier; I could nap during the day when my energy flagged and work at night when I couldn't sleep, and I only had to show my face at Brookhaven every few weeks.

I sent DOE one final request for help, although at this point I was convinced they would never help me. They were waiting for me to go away, presumably by dying, so I had nothing to lose by calling them out:

"Subject: Final notification of illness:

Gentlemen, this shall be the last e-mail you receive from me regarding the status of my health and subsequent requests for help in reaching some kind of viable arrangement for my continuance of work until OPM has finally reached a decision.

First, let me say that I have completed all necessary testing for final determination of undergoing a transplant operation (all of which was at my own expense)…This has been a long and painful road, the tests were sometimes painful and grueling. In the past seven months I have had over a thousand blood tests, one dozen IVs, an eight-hour Potassium drip, multiple Cat Scans, MRIs, and sonograms; I have even had a breast exam for cancer. I have undergone three nuclear medicine procedures, a diabetes test, a tuberculosis test, a gallbladder examination, Varices, duodenal ulcers, three PFTs, and at one point gave nineteen vials of blood all at one shot. The only test we have not done yet is a bone scraping.

It is to the point now where I have as many doctors as I take prescription meds such as Zoloft, Nexium, Inderal, Prednisone, Lactulose, Quinine, Xanax, Seroquel, Lasix, Aldacon, etc. Each med comes with its own remedy and its own side effects.

Now we come to the driving force behind this e-mail. I have repeatedly kept you informed as to my status, I have asked for the documentation you required, and I try to show up for work each day. This is a difficulty as I am prone to severe and debilitating cramping in my hands, feet, arms and legs. I also have on occasion passed out, but not before I was able to pull my truck off the road and stop (I woke about forty-five minutes later). I have asked management for assistance in coming up with some kind of solution whereby I could continue to work and yet stay closer to home. I am trying to get approval for telecommuting or possibly working at a federal facility closer to home. This truly seems like a management type function and one I should not be having to undertake alone. To inform me that I am either AWOL or in a Leave WO Pay status does nothing to help me except to magnify my already existing stress level. I don't know where to turn. When DOE asked me to respond to WTC and a subsequent other long-term deployment, I did not hesitate or waiver. I did my job; I did so believing that my government would always be there to support me.

I have been sorely let down. I have seen over the years how things can happen, almost overnight, when management has something to gain from it or it is something that they want. I am not a project or a program, I am a living human being in great pain and distress. Please help me get some relief. Why is it taking OPM so long, why can't I get reimbursed for monies I had to lay out for medical expenses, why can't I get my clearance restored, why wasn't I put on long-term disability?

P.S. If anyone takes offense at anything said here then maybe you need to take a good look inside yourself and ask if you did the right thing. I don't want to discuss this e-mail with anyone unless it is a solution to the issues I have laid out here.

Steven M. Centore"

But they never responded to this letter, either.

Eventually I wasn't allowed to drive and my doctors didn't want me in crowded places or traveling, so my options were limited. Sue drove me everywhere I needed to be and still managed to get herself to work every day. The seizures had mostly subsided, but they still happened, just less violently.

I finally received a Flexi-place Work Agreement (FWA) from the government which allowed me to work from home, but I still didn't have any real work. Shortly after that decision the management at Brookhaven informed me that DOE was considering layoffs, and since I wasn't really doing much at that point I'd be at the top of the list.

I had no pension yet, and a layoff would've meant no benefits as well. It didn't have to be me, of course, but why would management make any effort not to let me go? They hadn't had any use for me since I started complaining about being ill, so any excuse to get rid of me would serve their purposes.

I coped with everything as best I could by seeing a counselor, going to group therapy meetings and trying to understand what was happening to me. But most of that time is still a fog to me.

He still wasn't doing well with his work situation, and was very stressed going to work and dealing with DOE in any way, but his health was so precarious that it was difficult to piece together a solid case for disability benefits or disability retirement, so he kept plugging away at a place that had no use for his skills and no regard for his health. Going to work, which had for years been the focal point in his life, was an exercise in frustration.

After September 2006 when we finally found a suitable psychologist for Steve, the doctor would ask me over the phone how I was doing in the midst of this crisis. How was I handling the chaos and the strains from Steve's condition? Maybe it was because a psychologist was asking the question or that nobody else really pushed me before to think on it, but I immediately got all choked up. Everything had been about Steve for what seemed an eternity now, and I don't suppose I knew how I was handling it…perhaps I wasn't handling it very well at all.

I'd been on autopilot and was running in every direction putting out fires. "Nobody can understand just what it's been like, how much our lives have been destroyed since 9/11," I said. "We've been reminded of it every day since it happened. Everyone gets to move on and forget it, but it's in our faces constantly. Nobody can understand."

Other people had moved on, they were at barbeques with families and going to the movies and laughing at jokes. We were in a prolonged state of depression, Steve and I, including Steven Jr. (even when he eventually went away to college in Alabama). We were incapable of genuine happiness from 2001 on. Instead, we each adjusted in our own ways to what life had become in our house, and we each sought our own solace in whatever ways we could.

By this time Steve was retaining twenty to thirty pounds of water weight. His legs were so swollen, it looked like there was no distinction where his knees and ankles might be; his legs were more like tree trunks with no variation in width from top to bottom. You could poke into his leg and leave a half-inch indentation that remained for a long while after you stopped pressing.

He was also having frequent episodes of some physical imbalance that caused his body to emulate what seemed like low blood sugar, like a diabetic might have, only it wasn't confirmed he had blood sugar issues. He would slump on the couch and couldn't lift himself, could barely manage speaking, would sweat profusely and the surface of his skin felt like he was running a one hundred five-degree fever, yet a check of his internal temperature showed it to be normal/ With each of these episodes, he was nearing unconsciousness. He felt that sugar was what he needed, so I would try to feed him small pieces of chocolate, as difficult as it was for him to attempt to chew while he was near passing out.

We still don't know to this day if he was experiencing low blood sugar or if he was having continued ammonia level issues, and if the chocolate at the time was in fact doing anything at all, but we feel that it in fact kept him from passing out entirely. He had these attacks so frequently that we constantly traveled with candy and candy bars. He couldn't drive or really go anywhere by himself. These episodes continued throughout 2006, and Steve became better at sensing when they were coming on. It was just added to the list of screwed up, unexplained things that the doctors had yet to diagnose.

It was in this timeframe that we started to make contact with a group called "Unsung Heroes Helping Heroes" to find out if there were support groups or known medical care for people in Steve's situation who were experiencing poor mental and physical health from working at Ground Zero.

We attended a rally the group was involved with at Ground Zero and ran into one of the speakers who talked of her battles with a failing liver caused by being at Ground Zero. We got the name of her liver doctor who worked at NYU and made an appointment as soon as we could. We also had made contact with the NYU Transplant Center in New York City. The combination of these two contacts eventually led us to the conclusion that Steve indeed needed a liver transplant and he got his name of the waiting list in September 2006.

To that point my doctors weren't entirely sure what was wrong with me, but they were focused primarily on my gallbladder. The only thing they'd noted was wrong with my liver was that it had fatty deposits. That changed when I went to NYU, where the doctors told me my liver was now failing.

For a second opinion I visited Dr. Melissa Palmer, a renowned liver expert. "Your liver's shot," she told me. "You're going to need a liver transplant eventually."

I asked Dr. Palmer what caused my liver to fail so quickly, to which she informed me that while the alcohol was a part of it, certainly something from Ground Zero contributed to it. My liver should not have failed so quickly.

That was in the fall of 2006. I had no idea what "eventually" meant, but it came about much sooner than I expected.

Meanwhile I was asked to travel to Washington DC to testify before the House Education and Labor Committee. I'm still not sure if my name was in the database established by the Department of Health and Human Services for WTC responders or because a group called Unsung Heroes recommended me. But I was desperate to get help, and when I received the letter from Congressman Chris Shays to appear before the congressional subcommittee, I agreed to go.

CHAPTER 37

Testifying before a Congressional committee should have been intimidating, but I didn't feel I had anything left to lose. I thought I was going to die and the government had abandoned me. What did I have to lose by speaking my mind?

Politicians who participated in the hearing on Sept. 12, 2006 included Sens. Hillary Clinton and Charles E. Schumer, both of New York, and U.S. Reps. Carolyn Maloney, Jerrold Nadler and Anthony Weiner, all of whom had been outspoken on behalf of first responders with health issues.

The hearing was designed to spotlight the failures at every level of government to meet the needs of the first-responders, volunteers, recovery workers and residents, and to ensure that in the aftermath of future disasters the federal Occupational Safety and Health Administration (OSHA) would have a coherent national strategy if needed to protect workers in future emergencies.

"This is an extremely important subject, not just because thousands of 9/11 responders continue to suffer from the aftermath of that tragic event," said Rep. George Miller (D-CA), the chairman of the House Education and Labor Committee. "We need to make sure that first responders know that we will do everything we can to protect them during a national catastrophe like we faced as a result of terrorism six years ago and as a result of a hurricane two years ago."

"Last week Mt. Sinai (Hospital) released a report that confirmed our worst fears," said Sen. Clinton. "It confirmed an earlier report of the New York City fire department study. Tens of thousands of fire-fighters and all the others who were there were not only exposed but were suffering from significant medical and mental health problems. We're seeing young men and women in the prime of their lives who were in excellent physical health experiencing asthma, bronchitis, persistent sinusitis, laryngitis, and they are suffering from serious diseases, reactive airway disease, their lungs are collapsing, their livers are polluted. In fact, we are now seeing the first deaths."

Between April and June of 2006, doctors in the 9/11 workers' health program overseen by Mount Sinai saw two thousand three hundred twenty-three patients, said Dr. Philip Landrigan of the Mount Sinai School of Medicine. They found lower respiratory problems in forty percent of the patients and asthma and asthma-like reactive airways disease in thirty percent. Smaller portions of patients had chronic cough or chronic obstructive pulmonary disease. There were also upper respiratory conditions in fifty-nine percent. Mental health problems, the most common being post-traumatic stress disorder and depression, were seen in thirty-six percent of patients. Dr. Landrigan said it was still unclear how many of those patients will continue to experience such symptoms, or how many may develop new diseases like cancer many years after their exposure.

Other first responders told their stories, and I had the opportunity to tell mine. I wasn't dramatic; it's not my way. But I was honest about how I believed the government viewed my problems. First I addressed the government's analysis of post-9/11 data:

"When I finally did get a chance to participate with the two different organizations, I was well into obtaining my own care through my local doctors. I was also informed at the time that I would not be receiving treatment or reimbursement for my health problems. I realized at that point I was just a data point to the government and upon my death would become just another data point. I have received no help or aide from the government with my health.

My health insurance carrier and I have paid all my expenses, my portion of which was significant. I had to use my own sick and annual leave time to seek help from doctors that were able to help me. This has not only depleted all available leave time, but I had to borrow against my account and now am overdrawn on leave time.

So, in summing up issue one, I would say the programs are effective at doing what they were designed to do, gather historical data. However, they completely lacked any type of care or financial assistance for the truly injured federal responders."

And I also told them what the government should be doing instead:

"Realistically, the federal government needs to make every avenue of treatment available to its employees that have answered the call as requested by their government leaders. Idealistically, the federal government should provide training to the medical community concerning exposure to conditions that existed at Ground Zero. The local medical community, having little to no experience with situations and the conditions that existed at ground zero, are prone to shrug off non-traditional disease symptoms, which makes them susceptible to mis-diagnosing a patient.

While the second improvement would require significant amounts of time to put together and implement, the government could start by acknowledging that there are pertinent health effects due to exposure at Ground Zero.

I am a devout American patriot and a decorated veteran of the U.S. Armed Forces. I did what I did out of a sense of duty and pride. I currently suffer from a host of ailments, both physically and mentally, such as severe Post Traumatic Stress Disorder, Anxiety Disorder, as well as respiratory, gastrointestinal, and circulatory problems that make clear diagnoses and treatment difficult and often contradictory between different doctors. At best, it makes daily living a challenge.

Additionally, when requesting federal assistance such as Workman's Compensation or Disability Retirement, employees who are responsible for processing the claims seem to demonstrate a lack of training for dealing with individuals with severe PTSD or a multitude of as-not-yet properly diagnosed illnesses, and the injured employee is made to feel guilty for filing a claim. After having been diagnosed with severe PTSD symptoms over a year ago, and a flood of physical ailments soon afterwards, I still have not received any federal financial assistance for uncovered medical expenses or reimbursement of loss of all my leave time from work. I have had to take care of my own health and welfare issues instead of being backed by the federal government as promised. Immediate fair treatment is all that I am seeking for processing my claims for compensation and disability retirement."

Questioned about my gut response to the government's lack of response to problems, I was direct: "I feel like it's a contest to see if they're going to give in first or I'm going to die first."

Under the federal monitoring program, the first contact Steve had received about the program was in 2004, when a questionnaire was sent out. Steve filled out the questionnaire and was anxious to finally get some assistance for some of the health concerns he had by then, but as it turns out, the program did nothing but collect data and offered no assistance, or financial support. When asked by the subcommittee if the program was effective, he replied, "Well, if a program is designed to do nothing, and it does nothing, then, yes, I suppose it's effective."

Although he got a laugh out of the subcommittee and attendees, he unfortunately spoke the truth.

When former Senator Clinton stepped up to speak, she began by saying that she had no idea federal workers were being dealt with separately and then apologized directly to Steve for the disgraceful treatment by the U.S. government after Steve's many years of dedication and service. Afterwards, Senator Clinton came over to me, and shaking my hand, said she was sorry to hear of our struggles. She then shook Steve's hand and again apologized to him on behalf of the government. I got very choked up by this, as it was the first admission of fault by the government and the first validation for Steve that yes, he was an honorable, dutiful worker and that perhaps someone did in fact owe him an apology. It meant a great deal to us both that she had made this apology and that she was focusing her efforts, along with Senator Charles Schumer and Reps. Carolyn Maloney, Jerrold Nadler and Anthony Weiner, to rectify the wrongs on behalf of all the workers and residents working and living in and around Ground Zero.

I've been a lifelong Republican with no prior regard for the Clintons, but I have to admit that I was impressed with Hillary Clinton. She personally thanked me for my testimony and apologized for the way the government treated me. I cannot describe to you the feeling that I had at that moment when the former First Lady and now Senator from New York actually took the time to not only talk with me but thanked me for being a patriot. She knew the issues, she was there to advocate for first responders and she actually listened to me and the others when we spoke. For a day it felt as though someone was listening, that somehow my situation and the problems of all the others who were downtown after 9/11 might get some attention, at least long enough to address what was wrong with me and thousands of other first responders.

It was a short-lived feeling.

Sen. Clinton vowed to continue the fight for federal funds to treat sick 9/11 workers, but on Sept. 14 Senate Republicans sank the bill to provide $1.9 billion in Federal aid.

That felt like a betrayal, too.

A week later Sen. Clinton told reporters about my testimony, "One of the witnesses, Steve Centore, who was a federal employee, sat before us, his skin yellowed from the diseasing of his liver, his memory shot, his lungs collapsing and described in detail how his government has let him down and left him behind. If we don't take care of these people now and start putting up a system that we can have in place for the next several years, we are going to betray a fundamental responsibility to those whom we salute whenever it is convenient, whenever it is political. But enough with that. They don't want our speeches. They don't want our flowery rhetoric. They want our help."

But help would not be immediately forthcoming. Things would get far worse before they would get better.

CHAPTER 38

*B*y *February 2007, Steve's condition had gotten progressively worse. The medications could not control his malfunctioning liver and the excess fluids that continued to collect in his body as a result. He entered NYU Hospital on February 12 and stayed for a week while they removed thirty liters of fluids from him, drained through a large painful catheter inserted in the abdominal cavity near his stomach. He was released but had to re-enter NYU Hospital on March 12 to have yet another quickly accumulated thirty liters of fluid drained again. It was nearing the end of this stay that it was becoming evident that he might not be leaving the hospital this time.*

They were considering placing a stent in his liver to allow for blood flow through the liver, relieving the water retention issue, but this procedure is always a risky one, we were told by the doctors. By Wednesday, March 21, the decision was made for Steve that he had to wait in line for an immediate liver transplant, as his kidneys were starting to shut down as well as other organs.

The problem with getting on a liver transplant list is that because there are so few available organs, the only way to move to the top of the list is to get much sicker than everyone else. And I finally reached a point where I was near enough to death where they had moved me to the top of the list. I was so unlucky that I had lucked into the next available transplant.

The hypertension in my liver was causing veins to enlarge as the blood tried to find its way around the blockage in my liver. The danger was that any of the veins could rupture, killing me, so if the liver didn't fail first there was always the possibility that I'd suddenly bleed to death internally. Meanwhile, I was bleeding externally from every orifice.

While I was waiting for the liver transplant to come through, I shared a room with two guys. You get to know people in the hospital and you get to know their families, so it was hard to find out that neither of them were eligible for transplants because they had Hepatitis C. Liver failure with no hope of a transplant is a death sentence. As sick as I was and even though the jury was still out on whether I'd live long enough for the transplant, I still felt sorry for those two guys.

Around Valentine's Day I asked the doc if I could go down to the gift shop, but they told me I couldn't. Anytime you left the floor an orderly had to escort you either in a wheel chair or on a gurney. So, me being the wise guy, when the orderly took me to get an MRI, I asked him if we could stop at the gift shop. He was very reluctant at first but finally gave in to my insistent begging.

I asked him to buy a bouquet of flowers and a box of chocolates for me and put it on my account, which he did. I took the flowers and chocolates back to ICU with me and gave them to Sue who had been waiting for me to come back from my procedure. The nurses went berserk as you were not allowed to have real flowers in the ICU.

Oh well, it's the thought that counts.

Then came the day they told me my time had expired: if they didn't find a liver soon I wouldn't last another day. I accepted this news. What could I do about it? It was out of my hands.

Steve delivered the news to me over the phone that the transplant was happening as soon as they found a suitable donor, and although I heard him and understood, I didn't entirely process it. I planned to get into the city that day and was on the train by mid-morning. Then I got the call

*on the train from Steve asking where I was, and saying that he believed
they had found a liver for him.*

*My first reaction was sheer panic, though I kept it to myself and simply
told him I was on my way, and that I loved him. My eyes welled up and
I felt the fear rush over me, and then stopped myself and said, "You can't
do this, Sue…you can't fall apart in front of him." So I started praying
profusely, and called on any person I loved who has passed away that could
bring me comfort from the other side.*

*I hopped a cab from Penn Station to the East side to NYU Hospital
and while stopped at a traffic light, looked up at the building next to me,
and there in a window was a huge hand-written message painted on a
large plate-glass window that read "You R Loved"…I immediately felt a
rush of love wash over me, as if I'd gotten a direct message from heaven.*

*Then at the next stopped light, I looked again to the right at a brick
wall, and written across in script writing were the words "I Love You."
I began to cry and realized I was getting my answers from heaven. I
immediately felt a rush of reassurance and confidence that everything
would be alright.*

*I made my way to Steve's room and was beaming with excitement. I
was certain this liver was a gift from God and we were going to be okay.
I knew Steve was less convinced but I felt it in my bones.*

*I must have seemed like an overexcited cheerleader, as even the
doctor who was to perform the operation was questioning my unusual
excitement. But I just smiled brightly (perhaps slightly psychotically)
saying, "This is a great day…we've got a liver…everything's gonna be
great!"*

*By the time they were wheeling Steve away for his operation that
Thursday evening at five-thirty pm, I kissed him goodbye, but I fully
believed I would see him again. Only afterwards did I find out from Steve
that he didn't believe at all that he was going to make it, and that his kiss
to me was the last kiss of his life.*

The transplant surgeon, Dr. Lewis Teperman, and his staff somehow managed to keep me alive until they located a liver in Buffalo.
They boarded a helicopter, raced to Buffalo, harvested the organ and
rushed back.

As I was being prepped for my surgery, I began talking to this man
who was obviously Russian. To tease him, I called him Comrade. I
reminded him that, not long ago, his people were the enemy, that the

jury was still out, and that I'd spent my time in the navy playing cat-and-mouse with his countrymen.

"Do you know who I am?" he finally asked after listening to my taunts. I replied that I didn't. "Your anesthesiologist," he said.

Centore, I reminded myself, if you've learned nothing else in your life by now, it should be to keep your big mouth shut.

During the operation I dreamed I was wrapped in a shroud by something I couldn't see. I felt protected, so I asked this entity why it had saved me, among the millions of people it could have saved, and this entity replied that I had a purpose yet to serve in life. Everything in my life had happened for a purpose.

I told the entity I hoped the plans weren't for me to be a preacher. We have enough of them, it answered, and we can't control the ones we've got. That's when I knew that God had a sense of humor. The entity told me that, even though the answer might not be readily apparent, I would work it out inside myself.

Another transplant patient told me his donor had been in the room with him through the entire operation. Who knows what goes in our heads…maybe it's the anesthetic, but I know what I saw, and it was as real as anything I've ever seen.

I went under knowing I had made my peace with life, I'd taken care of everything I could take care of. It was beyond my control whether it was my time to cross over.

But it wasn't my time.

I felt so certain he would be okay that I insisted that nobody in my family or Steve's family needed to make the trip into the city that night during the ten-hour operation. I waited up all night by myself with the utmost confidence and by four-thirty in the morning I finally got to see him in the intensive care recovery room.

It was only when we made eye contact that I realized just what had transpired. He had tubes sticking out of his throat and neck, and he looking terrible. And then without the ability to speak, he made a few gestures that amounted to our version of "I love you" in sign language, and I got completely choked up and busted out in tears.

The emotional journey had come to a head. He had made it, and only now as I say this have I processed just what that meant. To this day, we are inseparable in spirit…he is my world.

CHAPTER 39

Immediately after surgery I was groggy and I couldn't speak, a result of the anesthetic, I was told, combined with having two tubes inserted in my throat for the past twelve hours. My first request was to see Sue, of course, but because I couldn't speak I had to use my hands to make myself understood. I made the universal hourglass shape for the orderly, Toby, but he just looked at me strangely. "You want me to get you a woman?" he asked.

Yes, I can barely move after a liver transplant, my guts are hanging out and I've got tubes stuck in me everywhere, but I want a woman, I thought. Jeez…Eventually, it occurred to Toby that I wanted a specific woman, namely my wife.

I'd done what I could not to burden Sue with my problems, not to tell her everything that was wrong and everything that could go wrong, mostly to no avail. She'd been there to tend to me all along, mostly by herself, and she was the first person I wanted to see. I told her before I went in that she was the last person I wanted to see, not believing that I was coming back. You see, I didn't tell Sue, or anyone for that matter, what the doctors had told me the night before. When I asked when I could go home, they informed me that I was slipping into renal failure and had only hours, maybe a day at most, to live. I didn't tell her because I knew that she would fret and without assurance that someone could be there with her, I opted to keep that bit of information to myself. Now that I realized I had made it and was in recovery, the first thing I wanted to do was see my best friend, Sue.

The following Monday morning, I was sitting in my bed watching the sun and the birds outside, laughing and crying at the same time, thanking God for showing me His grace and sparing my life. I could feel the presence of the Holy Spirit as it flooded into my body. A warmth came over me and completely enveloped me. Even though I was in and out of coherence, I was jubilant. I had made it! God had placed these events in my life in this sequence for a reason, even if I couldn't understand the reason, so I resolved to do something with the time that I had left.

One of those things would be to tell my story. The were several reasons why I wanted to do this, not because I want to embarrass anyone, but because I wanted my children and friends and family to understand what had happened to me and how I felt. I have been carrying such a weight of guilt believing that I had let my family down, my friends and co-workers down, my country down, and most of all, I let myself down. Letting myself down was becoming the hardest thing I had to live with. I began to worry when talking with some of my former DOE counterparts; I realized that they did not know what really happened to me, that somehow they had been given the impression that I was a screw-up and lucky to get anything from the government. That really bothered me to no end, so I decided a light needs to be shone on how the federal government has treated all of its workers post-9/11. It's not just me; there are thousands of Ground Zero workers in similar circumstances, some of whom are dying, and the fact that medical examiners are listing their deaths as being directly caused by 9/11 tells the public everything they need to know about the toxicity of the environment we were encouraged to work in, and were told was safe.

The doctors have advised me that the anti-rejection drugs will eventually wreak havoc with my other organs, so my time to do something with what's left of my life is probably limited. This has motivated me to help give a voice to those who aren't being heard, particularly the troops coming back from Iraq and Afghanistan, and to tell my story so people know that the people currently leading the country don't necessarily have the best interests of the common man at heart.

It's not just 9/11 first responders that have been jettisoned at the first sign of trouble; it's a consistent mechanism of the current administration to disavow or discredit anyone with a need or complaint, including the GIs coming back from Iraq; the alleged patriots in Congress consistently turn a deaf ear to properly funding medical care and benefits. But pretending we're not sick and injured and pretending we don't exist won't make us go away.

I respect the position, the office that politicians hold, but not necessarily the person holding that position, and I've come to believe that many of the people making decisions that affect the lives of service men and women, and the American people in general, aren't conscientious or qualified to make those decisions. Their lack of regard for the people who serve, and for the average American, must be brought to light.

I'm particularly sensitive to the dismissal by the federal government of PTSD claims, since mine was blatantly denied. The current administration has consistently declared veterans with PTSD claims (using operatives who are also psychiatrists of the American Enterprise Institute (AEI)) to attack the diagnosis of PSTD itself and malign the veterans afflicted with the disorder as "malingerers." For example, Cato Institute Senior Fellow Doug Bandow resigned on Dec. 15, 2005 after admitting he received funds from indicted lobbyist Jack Abramoff in exchange for op-ed pieces that decried government funding of PTSD treatment as money wasted on fraudulent claims. According to the administration's propaganda, the high incidence rate of PSTD among veterans is caused by personal defects or greed.

As for Ground Zero first responders, many are no better off. I got my reprieve with little time left to live, but others haven't been as fortunate. Illness and psychological damage goes unreported, undiagnosed and unfunded. I'm so grateful for the person who had the forethought to donate his organs, but there are many more first responders coming with similar or even worse problems.

My wife, Sue, keeps telling me I can't save the world, and she's right, but when I see things done purposefully wrong, or things that are unfair, it spurs me to act, and if not now, when?

The government, I've repeatedly and painfully learned, will always pat you on the back and say, "You're doing a great job, we're proud of you," but as soon as you complain or object they toss you aside. My life has been about service to my country, which was instilled in me from the time I was a little boy, and yet the times when I've needed assistance for problems I've developed in the service of my country the government has refused to help. It's beyond disillusioning.

It's time as a nation for us to realign our focus on what's important, and make Congress and the President and everyone with their heads stuck in the sand to take notice: the dirty work in the United States is in the hands of the few, and the least we owe those few is fair treatment when the dirty work is done. From Ground Zero to Walter Reed Hospital to hundreds of smaller hospitals across the globe, men and women who have put their lives on the line have been forgotten, and their complaints have been refused.

CHAPTER 40

After the transplant my middle son and his fiancée drove from his home in Ohio to Baltimore to meet up with my older son and his wife, and then they drove up to visit me for just an hour in the hospital. "I can't tell you I'm not touched, boys, but that's a long way to drive to see me for one hour," I told them.

My sons have a touch of the sympathetic in me that's also in them.

I don't know where it came from. My step-father, he was as un-emotional as they make them, and his father, my grandfather, was even more so. My step-father would have ordered us not to visit, and we would have obeyed him.

Within a few days I was out of intensive care and receiving visitors, and within a week I was sent home. You'd think with something as big as a liver transplant they'd keep you longer, but soon I was in my living room, surrounded by the TV, my laptop and piles of meds and attended to by Sue, who took a month off to work from home. I was a mess, with bandages that needed constant changing, tubes sticking out of me and fluids leaking all over the place, and she was my ever-present nurse and companion.

Within a month I was feeling better, probably better than I'd felt in years, and the doctors began removing the tubes and I gradually became more active.

In October 2006 the Department of Labor had recognized my Post Traumatic Stress Disorder claim (not coincidentally the least expensive portion of my medical bills), but rejected responsibility for my medical problems. I'm indebted to Congressman Tim Bishop, who was instrumental in pushing my paperwork through for worker's comp and disability retirement.

The following month the Office of Personnel Management determined that I was eligible to retire with a pension, but they disallowed my PTSD claim, leaving us with the lion's share of the bills to pay. Even today with a pension I pay for a large percentage of our medical care.

It makes you wonder, though, how one federal agency can approve a claim and another agency deny it? Aren't we all part of the same damn government?

Bureaucracy…

CHAPTER 41

I was well enough to attend former EPA secretary Christine Todd Whitman's hearing before Congress on June 25, 2007. Whitman was called to defend EPA's assurances that the air at Ground Zero was safe to breathe, and she was booed often as she tried to defend her statements about the air at Ground Zero in the weeks and months after 9/11.

Some people in the chamber were shouting during her testimony, but I wanted to hear what she had to say. After all, a host of politicians had made their quick appearances on the pile, but as EPA chief she was the one who had the data to back up her assurances that the air was safe to breathe.

Whitman repeatedly maintained that she and government officials warned those of us working on the pile to use respirators, while elsewhere in lower Manhattan the air was safe to the general public. Even if they had adequately warned those if us at Ground Zero (which they didn't) the rest is obviously false, because many residents have also developed respiratory problems.

"There are indeed people to blame. They are the terrorists who attacked the United States," she said, basically ignoring the accusations.

The hearing was called by Rep. Jerry Nadler, a Democrat whose district includes the World Trade Center site and one of the politicians leading the charge for the government to accept responsibility for what happened to the workers at Ground Zero. Nadler said the Bush administration "has continued to make false, misleading and inaccurate statements and refused to take remedial actions, even in the face of overwhelming evidence."

No one who actually worked the pile bought her testimony, and there was plenty of noise when Whitman said former Mayor Rudy Giuliani's administration "did absolutely everything in its power to do what was right" in handling the health concerns. Giuliani may be America's mayor after 9/11, but there was plenty wrong with 9/11 and what happened in its aftermath that can be laid right at Giuliani's feet.

The government's air analysis still hasn't been released, but what's known about the air at Ground Zero is bad enough. The thousands of tons of toxic debris resulting from the collapse of the Twin Towers consisted of more than twenty-five hundred contaminants, including non-fibrous material and construction debris, glass and other fibers, cellulose and asbestos, lead and mercury. There were also unprecedented levels of dioxin and Polycyclic aromatic hydrocarbons (PAHs) from the fires which burned for more than three months. Some of the substances, including crystalline silica, lead, cadmium and PAHs are carcinogenic, while other substances can trigger kidney, heart, liver and nervous system damage.

President Bush has been faulted by some for interfering with the EPA interpretations and pronouncements regarding air quality, though Whitman has remained loyal to the party even after leaving the administration. Giuliani has been faulted for urging financial industry personnel to return to Wall Street and for encouraging a competitive atmosphere between firefighters and cops that may have led to unnecessary first responder deaths.

A 2003 report by the EPA's inspector general said that Whitman's assurances about air quality on Sept. 18, 2001, were misleading, since when the statements were made the EPA didn't have sufficient data and analysis to justify them; the report also said that the White House had convinced EPA to add reassuring statements and delete cautionary ones.

During the cleanup efforts the EPA did eventually provide thousands of respirators for workers to wear during their efforts.

On Feb. 2, 2006, a U.S. District Court judge rejected Whitman's request for immunity in a class action lawsuit brought by a group who claimed exposure to hazardous debris from the collapse of the World Trade Center. The judge stated, "No reasonable person would have thought that telling thousands of people that it was safe to return to lower Manhattan, while knowing that such return could pose long-term health risks and other dire consequences, was conduct sanctioned by our laws," and called Whitman's actions "conscience-shocking."

"Initial exposures were basically a blackout—exposures people will, cumulatively, never see in a lifetime again," said Paul Lioy, of the Environmental and Occupation Health Sciences Institute of the University of Medicine in New Jersey. "The problem we have now is we don't know the long-term, lifetime, health consequences. We just don't know."

In 2003 Congress passed the Consolidated Appropriations Resolution, which made an additional $90,000,000 available for administering "baseline and follow-up screening and clinical examinations and long-term health monitoring and analysis for emergency services personnel and rescue and recovery personnel, of which not less than $25,000,000 shall be made available for such services for current and retired firefighters." The funding was distributed through NIOSH in the form of eight grants to the New York City Fire Department (FDNY), the Mount Sinai Center for Occupational and Environmental Medicine and six other centers in and around New York City to establish a five-year health screening program for rescue workers.

None of the funds were made directly available to employees of the federal government. NONE!

Six years after 9/11 in September 2007, I was featured along with other first responders in a *Discover* magazine story titled, "The 9/11 Cover-Up," written by Michael Mason. Several New York politicians, including Congressman Jerry Nadler, supported the story's conclusions, but those politicians have been in the minority. The federal government continues to pretend nothing went wrong and the sick and dying first responders don't exist.

And eventually, if they wait long enough, they'll be correct.

CHAPTER 42

These days I take nearly thirty pills every day, including anti-rejection drugs and blood pressure and asthma meds, and there's always the fear in the back of my mind that my body will ultimately reject the liver and I'll be in dire straits once more. But for now I'm alive, I feel better than I have in years, and I intend to use whatever time I have left well.

Steve had to let go eventually of his resentment of the people who abandoned him because he couldn't handle the psychological damage of never letting go of it. I, however, will always hold DOE and the U.S. government accountable for Steve's illnesses, because I was the one who had to watch my husband slowly turn into a walking corpse in the years since 9/11.

And to find out in 2006 just how much we were deceived about the toxic exposure at Ground Zero when Steve had spent four months there, with the first week or so on round-the-clock duty there wearing nothing but a paper face mask, which he couldn't even wear most of the time because it was constantly clogged with dust.

Steve never had a chance to de-stress from Ground Zero, but kept on with life- threatening work with constant reminders of all the people he personally knew who were now dead, with grimness and death being a steady cancer eating at him. The only thing that kept him above the water was the honor of doing his duty. It was important work in anyone's eyes, except for his direct management. When DOE stripped the honor of doing his job from him, the job that defined so much of who he was, he died inside. He had absolutely nothing left. DOE and the government as a whole had successfully stripped down this man to an empty shell. And here I was with the remnants.

I have seen his soul stripped down to the bone, I have witnessed his deepest fears, I have cried the deepest tears with him, we have been driven to the edge together clinging to each other, and now we have been brought full circle with hope for a future together.

I'm not sure what the future will continue to bring for Steve in terms of his health. We already are on to the next problem, his asthma, a condition he never had before 9/11. But we have hope that we can resolve or at least manage it, and at the very least we know we have each other.

I'm not demonstrative by nature; I was raised to be stoic and not to complain. Men didn't share their feelings in those days and certainly not in the military culture I was raised in. It went against everything I felt and believed in to ask for help, and to cast blame when no help was forthcoming. I would've been content to do my job and remain invisible to the public, running all over the northeast seeking out radioactive hot spots and looking for terrorists. All I ever wanted to do was serve, quietly. Circumstances beyond my control made that mission impossible, and I didn't raise my voice until they turned their backs on me.

And if feelings are hurt in the telling of this story, so be it. It's my life, it's all true, and if anyone is embarrassed by how they're portrayed they probably should be. If anything, I've shown restraint.

Recently I went to Brookhaven lab to return some old equipment I had found stashed away in one of my boxes from my old office. It was my first visit since my health spiraled out of control. When I arrived I met up with the guy who took my place as the Regional Coordinator. He was very condescending and openly aggressive toward me as we exchanged items; he treated me as though I was a terrorist suspect.

I guess what bothered me most was the fact that this same guy was fired from his last position within DOE's counterintelligence program for being too arrogant. *How in the hell do you get fired for being too arrogant working with a group of people known for their arrogance?* I wondered. But, I brushed it off, made the exchange and went home believing that somehow karma will definitely have a role to play here.

On a positive note, the following weekend, Oct. 5, 2007, I attended a reunion with my brothers from the Seahorse. God knows I did not want to leave that place. Some of my bros reminded me, after hearing my story, that I am not alone in the world, and that they were always with me. I slept very soundly that night, comforted in the thought that after almost thirty years apart, my brothers had not forgotten me.

Also during this time my second grandson, Jaxon Cross Centore was born. Now he and my first grandson, Dante Xavier Centore would become a major part of my new world.

I suppose my ability to enjoy the little things and focus on what matters most indicates that my life is returning to some semblance of normal, something it hasn't been since Sept. 11, 2001. My weekly doctor visits recently became quarterly; soon they'll be yearly. I take a lot of medication, but despite that I feel better than I have in years, and I'm driving again. My life, and Sue's life, has a clarity and quality that had been missing for so long.

It was June 2007, two months after Steve's liver transplant, and my brother Ken was over and he, Steve, my sister-in-law Marie and I were all talking, having a good time, and I let out a big laugh and sang a little ditty that I often do.

Ken gave me this quirky little smile.

"What?" I asked.

"You know, you used to do that all the time, laughing out loud and doing your little song thing," he commented. "I haven't heard you do that for years. It sounds good.

Welcome back."

I still don't know what God wants me to do with the rest of my life, and maybe it'll never be apparent. I've been through a lot, but for the first time in years I see hope for the future, and for the first time in years I see that same hope in Sue's eyes. I know, from this point forward, regardless of what happens, we'll be all right.

Addendum

The New York City Department of Health and Mental Hygiene (DOHMH), the federal Agency for Toxic Substances and Disease Registry (ATSDR), and the Federal Emergency Management Agency (FEMA) have established the World Trade Center Health Registry to track the physical and mental health problems of people exposed to the fire and smoke caused by the destruction of the World Trade Center towers. The registry is open to up to two hundred thousand people who were living south of Canal Street on 9/11/01, students and staff at schools or day care centers south of Canal Street, workers involved in the rescue, recovery, or clean up at the WTC site or WTC recovery operations on Staten Island between 9/11/01 and 6/30/02, as well as those people who were in a building, on the street, or on the subway south of Chambers street on 9/11/01.

More than fifty thousand people have enrolled in the registrythus far atwww.nyc.gov/html/doh/html/wtc/index. People who join the registry are interviewed about their exact location on September 11, 2001, their exposure to smoke and dust and any health problems suffered since. Registrants will be periodically contacted by the New York City DOHMH to monitor any changes in health. This information will be compared with the general population in order to identify any health problems linked to September 11, 2001.

Those interested in pushing the federal government to release the data collected at Ground Zero can contact 9/11 ENVIRONMENTAL ACTION, a community-based organization of residents, parents and occupational safety, public and environmental health advocates formed in April 2002 to end the federal Environmental Protection Agency cover-up. 9/11 EA fights for a comprehensive clean-up and demands medical monitoring and health care for everyone harmed by WTC contamination. The organization is a 501(c)(3) nonprofit organization, and all contributions are tax deductible in accordance with IRS regulations.

Contact them at:
9/11 Environmental Action
P.O. Box 250192
Columbia University Station
New York, NY 10025

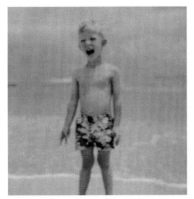

Fun in the sun and living in
Hawaii.

Age five in East Meadow,
Long Island, NY.

In Ft. Macon, NC, at eighteen months

Freshman year of high
school in Millington, TN. I
was in Navy JROTC.

High school graduation picture,
Havelock, NC, 1975.

USS Seahorse (SSN-669)—
The Pride of the Fleet.

Boot camp picture, taken next to my
bunk in our barracks.

My re-enlistment ceremony in
Roosevelt Roads, PR.
The skipper gave each man
re-enlisting his choice of
where he wanted the
ceremony to be held. I chose a
rubber raft over the side
(note the jazzy "underway"
space patrol helmet).

Award ceremony, dockside in Charleston, SC. Captain Henry
McKinney is seen awarding me my submarine qualification pin
(otherwise known as "dolphins"). The Seahorse is in the background.

My three children from my first marriage: Christina, Chuck, and Court.

My second son, Courtney, did a hitch in the Marine Corps *(Semper Fi)*.

My oldest son, Charles, who became an officer onboard Navy submarines.

Chuck and Steven, Jr. onboard the USS Corpus Christie.

Steven, Jr. in Navy JROTC in Riverhead High School, Riverhead, NY.

Sue and I on an early date at Okey Dokey's.

September 2001, grabbing some water in front of the NASDAQ. The sign says, "Hot Food at St. Paul's." In the very early days there wasn't any food or water; however, the local folks brought us bottled water and lunches in brown paper bags with messages of encouragement on them. Mine said, "May God Bless You."

Ground Zero: instrument checks at our "command post" which we set up at the corner of Chambers and West Streets, NYC.

Ground Zero: The smoke plume would block out the sun in the middle of the day. Note the sun trying to peek in through the clouds.

All that was left of one of the towers. Note the windows blown out in the structure in the background.

In the early weeks, this is what it was like to work around Ground Zero. That is tower seven in the background. Note the dust on the street.

There was dust everywhere, which made it feel surreal, almost like walking on the moon. Note the papers everywhere; they came off of desks that were in the towers.

Weeks later and the smoke was still coming off the pile.

On my very last tour of my last day, I bumped into my cousin, John Bergquist, who was a Lieutenant in the NYPD at the time.

A moment of memory loss during my testimony before Congress, September, 2006.

Official wedding day for Sue and me at the Riverhead United Methodist Church in Riverhead, NY, July 5, 2003.

Christmas day at Chuck and Frankie's home, December 2005. I am holding my grandson, Dante. Note my discoloration.

Christmas day at my in-laws' home, December 2006. The illness is really starting to ravage my body.

Grandpa (me) and Jaxon Cross, Courtney and Lana's son, taken September 2007. Note the improvement in my color and appearance.

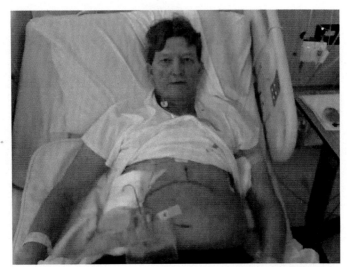

Snagged from the jaws of death; after my surgery in March 2007.

At Ground Zero during a press conference in September 2007 with Congressman Nadler, Congresswoman Maloney and *Discover* magazine CEO Bob Guccione, Jr. I am in the back.